THE ILLEGALS

Also by Grace Halsell

Peru
Soul Sister
Evers
Black White Sex
Bessie Yellowhair
Los Viejos

GRACE HALSELL

THE ILLEGALS

A JOHN L. HOCHMANN BOOK

STEIN AND DAY/*Publishers*/New York

First published in 1978
Copyright © 1978 by Grace Halsell
All rights reserved
Designed by Karen Bernath
Printed in the United States of America
Stein and Day/*Publishers*/Scarborough House,
Briarcliff Manor, N.Y. 10510

A John L. Hochmann Book

Library of Congress Cataloging in Publication Data

Halsell, Grace.
  The illegals.

  Includes index.
  1. Mexicans in the United States—Social conditions.
2. Migrant labor—United States. 3. Aliens—United
States. I. Title.
E184.M5H34   331.5′44′0973   77-25020
ISBN 0-8128-2464-4

DEDICATED
TO THE
MANY FRIENDS
I FOUND
ALONG THE
BORDER

CONTENTS

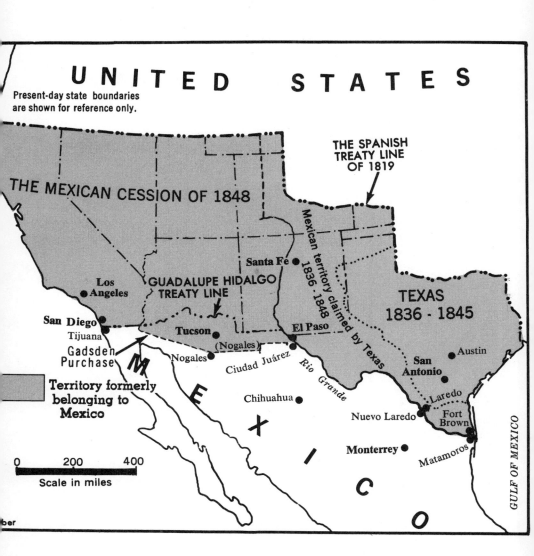

The War on Our Doorstep

On the southwest border of the United States a war is being waged—a war to which the weapons, techniques, and even some of the personnel of Vietnam have been transplanted, and which seems to have as little chance of success. It is a war to hold back a tide of brown people—Mexicans—driven by hunger and unemployment and lured by tales of affluence in a Promised Land only a bus ride away to the north.

The tales come from those who move back and forth across the border, bringing to their slum *barrios* and pueblos reports akin to the "gold in the streets" that once beckoned hordes of immigrants from Europe. And they come from the U.S. mass media, which infiltrate into their hovels depicting a life of material plenty in *el norte* that Mexicans find in irresistible contrast with the poverty around them.

But if this suggests the great era of European immigration, there is a difference: the Europeans could come in legally, unhampered by quotas. Most Mexican immigrants, however, are illegal—"undocumented," as the government euphemistically puts it. In its war effort against the illegals, the United States has flung men, weapons, and dollars into fruitless tactics to stanch the flow. The war has demanded the attention of Presidents, cabinet members, legislators, other high officials, and the TV and print media. It is a war that influences all our daily life—the food we eat, the education of our children, the language we speak, the taxes we pay. It is a war of mercenaries against a people expressing their instinct to survive. It is a grim game of life, death, and desperation which both sides realize can never be won as it now is being waged.

To see at first hand the waging of this war and what it means to those trapped in it, I traveled back and forth along the 2,000 miles of our border with Mexico, living first on one side and then on the other. On the United States side, I cruised in souped-up vehicles with armed Border Patrolmen as they vainly attempted to seal our porous border. I became a "wetback" swimming the Rio Grande with a Mexican peasant. I dodged the ambush of Border Patrol guards with undocumented domestics. A third time I sneaked across with a smuggler who guides illegals from Tijuana into San Diego.

There are now six, ten, or twelve million illegals—no one knows the exact number—living in the United States, most of them having come here in the past ten years. There are as many of them now as those who came to this country *legally* from everywhere in the world between 1900 and 1910, the peak period of our immigration. The illegals come from every country in the world. But we apprehend a larger proportion of brown-skinned Mexicans than white Canadian or European aliens because the Mexicans are easier to identify.

We train and equip an army of men, many veterans of our bigger Southeast Asian wars, not for apprehending *all* illegals but for the sole purpose of apprehending Mexican illegals. Our Border Patrol boggles our minds with its statistics—all about Mexicans. It claims to arrest three thousand Mexican illegals each day. But these figures are designed to dazzle us and hide the truth, like the "body count" in Vietnam. Over 90 percent of those arrested are recycled—that is, sent back to Mexico the same day—and they appear in the statistics again and again. Whatever the precise number of illegal Mexicans, however, we know they represent a problem that will demand our attention for many years to come.

By a conservative estimate, we spend about $250 million each year to wage the war on our doorstep. Public sentiment backs this war. Seventy-two percent of United States citizens, according to a September, 1977, Gallup poll, favored making it against the law to employ illegals. Labor leaders, politicians, and spokesmen for taxpayers have said the illegals are responsible for unemployment and the deficit in our balance of payments and that they drain off a disproportionate share of our welfare services.

Zero Population Growth, a national organization that advocates world population stabilization, says the illegals "depress wages, displace low-skilled American workers, drive unemployed workers to seek assistance from social-service programs. Furthermore," the organization warns, "they have a negative effect on our balance of payments, inasmuch as they typically remit funds to family members in the home country. They certainly do nothing to enhance environmental quality because they increase crowding and add to the burden on water, energy and sanitation facilities."

Former generals who have run the Immigration Service and the Border Patrol espoused the same views. One of these former commissioners, one-time Marine General Leonard Chapman, said illegal Mexican workers are "a major threat to our nation and our way of life." He declared, "If we could locate and deport the three to four million illegals who currently hold jobs in the United States, replacing them with citizens and legal residents, we could reduce our own unemployment dramatically—as much as 50 percent."

In 1977 President Carter named a Mexican American, Leonel Castillo, former Houston City Controller, as Commissioner of the Immigration and Naturalization Service in the Justice Department. He has sought to bring a greater awareness of civil rights to the paramilitary Border Patrol for which he is responsible. But most of the agents with whom I talked still adhere to General Chapman's "war" philosophy: We are being "invaded" by a rising brown tide and unless this enemy is eradicated we will be engulfed, overwhelmed, and defeated.

The Mexicans have a saying—"So far from God, and so close to the United States." It is the key to much of their history and their present dilemma.

Texas, California, New Mexico most of Arizona, a piece of Wyoming, and large parts of Nevada, Utah, and Colorado were acquired as a result of a war against Mexico. What is happening in Mexico now has to be understood in the context of that war.

By the time the United States began the war, in 1846, the existence of gold in California was well known. By taking California from Mexico, as well as all the land between it and the United States, we could extend this nation to the Pacific—and we called this our "manifest destiny."

President James K. Polk sent United States troops, under the command of General Winfield Scott, to Texas. Ulysses S. Grant, who served as a second lieutenant in the war, said in his memoirs "we were sent to provoke a fight." He called it a "political war" and wrote that it was "one of the most unjust ever waged by a stronger against a weaker nation."

Our volunteer troops "committed atrocities to make
Heaven weep and every American of Christian morals
blush for his country," General Scott later reported.
"Murder, robbery and rape of mothers and daughters in
the presence of tied-up males of the families have been
common all along the Rio Grande." George G. Meade,
then a lieutenant but later a Civil War general, said the
U.S. volunteers were "driving husbands out of houses and
raping their wives. ... They ... are a set of Goths and
Vandals without discipline, making us a terror to innocent people."

Religion played its role. Our invading troops were for
the most part Protestants and gave vent to their strong
anti-Catholic feelings by, as one witness said, "sleeping
in the niches devoted to the sacred dead ... drinking out
of holy vessels." Two hundred and fifty American troops,
mostly of Catholic background, deserted and joined the
Mexicans in attempting to defend their land. Other
United States troops captured them, however, and ex-
ecuted them in a small town called San Angel.

Many others who now are our heroes opposed this war.
Thoreau went to jail rather than pay taxes to support it.
Abraham Lincoln, when he was a freshman Congressman, accused Polk of ordering U.S. troops "into the midst
of a peaceful Mexican settlement, purposely to bring on a
war ... and has swept *on* and *on*. ..."

The Treaty of Guadalupe Hidalgo in 1848 ended our
war against Mexico. For almost half of Mexico we paid
$15 million, less than you would pay for a downtown Los
Angeles hotel today. Nine days before the treaty was
signed a new discovery of gold in California was
announced.

We not only annexed land, we acquired the Mexican
citizens who lived in what is now the U.S. Southwest. One
day they were Mexicans living in Mexico, and the next
they were Mexican Americans. By treaty we guaranteed
them many rights and privileges, including the right to

retain their customs and language. But we imposed on them a new body of law, a new language, a new economy, and a new culture. Like the American Indians, they were a minority annexed by conquest.

Though this country reaped wealth from the empire it gained, Mexicans have continued to relive their tragedy. They observe the anniversaries of their defeat in the battles of Chapultepec and Molino del Rey as national days of fasting and prayer. And as late as 1943 Mexican schools still used maps designating the land we acquired as "territory temporarily in the hands of the United States."

With a new empire to be developed and a labor shortage created by the Civil War, the United States began importing the poor of the world—Chinese, Irish, Italians, and Mexicans—to put down railroad tracks and to work in the fields.

The nearest were the Mexicans. They lived in extreme rural poverty, and we had money and jobs to offer. Unlike the Asians and the Europeans, they rarely brought their families to the United States and they could easily be deported.

The influx of contract laborers from Mexico increased sharply during World War I. In this period, we opened the doors so that Mexican laborers could work in the fields and maintain the railroads. But, by law, we made it plain we wanted them as laborers, not as settlers or potential citizens.

With our sudden entry into World War II, the United States government, complying with the demands of U.S. growers, initiated and supervised a program to recruit tens of thousands of Mexican laborers called "braceros" for work in this country.

Between 1950 and 1960, more than three million Mexicans worked in more than 20 states. For the growers the program was a dream: a seemingly endless army of cheap, unorganized workers brought to their doorstep by the government. United States employers benefitted from a risk-free pool of menial labor. They paid no social security, fringe benefits, insurance, or hospitalization. And they determined all the working conditions: hours, wages and living accommodations. Over a 22-year period, we imported a total of five million laborers.

Under public pressure from labor unions, Congress voted in December, 1964, not to renew the bracero program. More than two hundred thousand Mexican workers were abruptly expelled from the United States. They had jobs one day. They were told to go home the next.

"When it ended, all the braceros went home," a quip goes, "and came back as illegals."

Employers still wanted Mexican labor, and the Mexicans were still desperate to work. Moreover, after more than two decades of traveling as regular commuters to *el norte*, they knew the way and continued to come as illegals after the bracero program was ended.

I interviewed scores of these illegals in jails, prisons, and detention centers in many parts of the United States. All said: "I came here to work. I have done nothing wrong." They have a minimum of schooling. They have very little money. They rarely speak English. They have only the clothes on their backs, the will to survive, and faith that in *el norte* they can find work. "I heard about this country when I was ten years old," a Mexican being held at the El Paso Federal Detention Center told me. "My father came here as a bracero. And he told me there were many factories here so I knew there would be many jobs." He said he could earn ten times as much here as he could in Mexico—and in Mexico there was no work anyway.

With sixty-three million people, Mexico is now the world's tenth most populous nation. Mexico has an estimated growth rate of 3.5 percent a year, higher than India's, and the population will double in 20 years. Within the next 45 years, if current trends continue, Mexico will have more people than there now are in the United States.

Mexico City has 20 percent of the country's population, but 35.6 percent of its industry, 41.2 percent of its commerce, and 50.1 percent of its services.

Each year, five hundred thousand peasants give up trying to survive in the countryside and converge on Mexico City where there are already twelve million persons. They build makeshift hovels and search for jobs.

Projections by the United Nations foresee a city of twenty million by 1985 and thirty-one million by the turn of the century. Some experts predict an explosion long before either figure is reached. With four million peasants still landless, extensive rural and urban poverty, and too sharp a division between the very rich and the very poor, leftist firebrands have ready tinder. The Communist Party expects for the first time to field candidates in the 1979 congressional elections.

Mexico is a nation of young people: Almost half the population is under 15 years of age, and soon they will come into a labor force already burdened with unemployment and marginal employment. Over 48 percent—8.5 million of the 17.5 million persons in the labor force—now are estimated to be unemployed or marginally employed.

It's a question of whether elected officials can move fast enough.

The economy creates only about one hundred fifty thousand new jobs each year of the four hundred thousand that are needed.

Seventeen percent of the population earns less than $75 a year. Moreover, inflation now is running at an explosive rate of 30 percent. For the U.S. tourist the devaluation of the *peso* means he can buy more for his dollars. For the poor Mexican, the devaluation means that prices have doubled while his pay—if he is lucky enough to have a job—has not increased proportionately.

Probably no nation has moved more quickly than Mexico from an agricultural base to industrialization. But more than half of Mexico's workers still are small farmers or landless peasants. The heart of Mexico's problem lies in its rural villages, where its most serious poverty exists. Agriculture in the most remote areas has not changed in the four hundred years since the Spanish Conquest.

Big farming, meanwhile, has become big business in Mexico with the influx of the multinational corporations based in the United States. They produce an estimated half to two-thirds of the fresh fruits and vegetables consumed in the United States during the winter months. Two of these growers control over 90 percent of Mexican asparagus production. Increasingly, Mexican land is being used to produce specialized crops—strawberries, tomatoes, melons—for export to the United States. Meanwhile, there is not enough production of basic foods such as corn for Mexico's hungry millions.

"When there is hunger, there is revolution," a Mexican Secretary of Labor has said. Starving peasants on remote mountains can do little to attract our attention, but they now are in Mexico City and they can light fires to burn the offices and homes of those who do not give them jobs. We in the United States, like the Mexican officials, are sitting on top of a Mexican volcano. It has not erupted by 1978 for one reason: the "hopeless" have one last hope: a job in *el norte*. We provide the safety valve that allows Mexico's officials to buy time and create jobs that can prevent a revolution by millions of hungry people.

It was to discuss their positions, atop the volcano, that President Carter and President José López Portillo met in early 1977 in Washington, D.C.

López Portillo spoke frankly of Yankee imperialism. He's willing to forget our nineteenth-century imperialism that took half of Mexico. We must deal today, he said, with economic imperialism. He pleaded with the United States to allow Mexico to export "products—not men." He asked us to lower trade and tariff barriers to allow Mexican exports easier access to U.S. markets. Both he and the multinational corporations want this. But our labor unions and domestic manufacturers do not want foreign competition. And congressmen who control trade barriers represent their constituencies.

The Carter Administration has indicated that a mammoth aid program, much like the Marshall Plan for Europe at the end of World War II, is being considered for Mexico. But to get such aid through Congress, the Administration would have to agree that much of the money would be spent for goods we would export. This would be a bonanza for United States export industries and their workers, but do little for Mexican employment. It would be a heavy price for Mexico to pay for United States "aid."

Meanwhile, newly confirmed Mexican oil reserves will figure prominently in all of our future negotiations with Mexico.

By 1982, Petroleos Mexicanos, the country's oil monopoly, expects to be exporting 1.1 million barrels a day, worth some $5.5 billion a year at current prices. An 800-mile pipeline could feed more than two billion cubic feet of natural gas a day across the United States border, adding $1.9 billion a year to Mexico's accounts.

Large international oil companies, many based in the United States, are expected to bargain with fervor to develop Mexico's great potential. No one knows how large Mexican resources are, but some estimates place them second only to Saudi Arabia's.

The Mexicans hope the United States will look to Mexico as a future source of oil. And our banks, desperate for good international loans, are eager to finance the development of Mexican oil imports.

But it will be a long time before landless Mexican peasants will benefit from this. In the meantime, they will continue to come to this Promised Land for work.

II

Swimming to the Promised Land

As I traveled along our 2,000-mile border with Mexico I thought about how and where to experience best what an illegal must feel in swimming the Rio Grande to the United States. In the Rio Grande Valley of Texas I visited with Antonio Orendáin, a native of the state of Jalisco in Mexico and now an organizer of Texas farm workers. A strong, husky man who looks like the Mexican hero, Zapata, Orendáin told me he first crossed illegally about 1951 when he was 18. Eventually he met and married Raquel, a Mexican American. Her legal status facilitated his citizenship but by no means made it automatic.

In a decade of undocumented status, he would cross, get arrested, and be deported to Mexico. Orendáin said he crossed over at least 22 times, using a different alias each time the police picked him up. His surname Orendáin was so unusual it was suspect, he said, so he used names that were easier for the police to write—Rivera, Pérez, or Gómez.

Once, he said, he came over illegally five times in one day. "Each time I was stopped by a different Border Patrolman. And each time I gave a different name. He'd say, 'Is this your first time?' They don't usually put you in jail—right here along the border—for one crossing, so I'd say yes. And he'd throw me back to Mexico. Then I'd swim over again." The fifth time no one caught him and he kept going to California.

"Even when I got married to Raquel, I used an alias," Orendáin told me. "She was an American citizen but I was still illegal." They were married in 1953, and he got his citizenship in 1959.

After Orendáin had driven me to his trailer home in San Juan, Texas, and introduced me to Raquel, I asked him to show me where he swam the Rio Grande as an illegal. We drove a few miles from his home to a place where I could see that only the river separated the Texas town of Hidalgo from Reynosa, in Mexico. Our border with Mexico has a dozen sets of these twin cities, more than along any other international frontier.

From an embankment along the river we watched the surging brown waters below.

"If you swim over from Mexico," Orendáin explained, a grin beneath his expansive moustache, "You arrive here wet—*mojado*." The term applies today, he said, to any illegal: "Maybe you walk across a desert, but if you don't have papers they still call you a wet, or a wetback."

Orendáin estimated the river before us to be about 200 feet wide. It can be swift and unpredictable, and after heavy rains, he said, "I've seen it when it's 4 miles wide."

Mexicans always have lived on either side of the river, viewing it as a mystical god to be placated with prayers, respected, and held in awe.

"You think you know that river, but you never do,"
Orendáin reflected. "Once I left Mexico to swim to the
United States. I could see the shoreline and I was
swimming north. Eventually I reached land—hoping I
would not be arrested—and quietly sneaked ashore—only
to discover I was still in Mexico! The river can be that
circuitous."

Rising high in the mountains of southern Colorado, the
Rio Grande flows southward through the center of New
Mexico, then enters the Texas desert at El Paso. It
courses its way for 1,000 miles in Texas down to
Brownsville in the Gulf of Mexico—providing half the
length of our border with Mexico. The United States and
Mexico have shared in the construction of two dams along
the Rio Grande: one, Falcon, between McAllen and
Laredo; the other, Amistad (Friendship), near Del Rio.
The cost of the dams has been offset by the flood damage
they have prevented. In addition, they have provided a
steady supply of water for municipal purposes and
irrigate several million acres in both countries. Both
countries freely make public use of the reservoirs.

I had visited both the dams, but now with Orendáin I
was getting close enough to touch the waters of the river
and wade in them. He and I scrambled down the steep
embankment and sat on our haunches in the sand. He
related more details of one crossing: "See all those holes
in the embankment? Once I crossed at night and slept in
a hole like that. Then, about 4:00 A.M. I started walking,
hoping the police wouldn't see me, but they did." Orendáin points to a small plastic bag discarded in the sand.
"You use one of those little bags to carry your clothes
when you're swimming," he explains. Once on shore, the
illegal takes dry shoes, pants, and shirt from the bag and
goes on by land.

I imagine the illegal climbing up the steep embankment. For a few moments he will feel himself sheltered

by the trees and brush, but at any moment he can expect a Border Patrol agent to grab him. He will live every moment in fear. He can never breathe freely, normally.

The muddy waters appear placid. I look up and down and across the river. I see no one else on either bank. I have not yet worked up the courage to tell Orendáin that I want to swim across. Instead, like a child who needs to brag to bolster a flagging will, I tell him that I *could* swim across.

"The river may look calm," he replies. "But the currents can be dangerous. Eddies and undertows can pull you under. Sometimes it goes wild, uproots trees, sweeps people, cattle, and houses downstream, demolishes bridges. Flash floods tore down a big steel bridge between Laredo and Nuevo Laredo. So you never know about that river." Then he adds: "And besides—you can get shot."

Does he really believe, I ask, that Mexicans still are shot?

"Yes," he replies, "We find the dead bodies in the fields and in the river. 'Rednecks' have shot *many* Mexicans. It's a sport, even a laughing matter with them." One example was the legendary Texas gunman King Fisher. When asked how many notches he had on his gun he replied: "Thirty-seven—not counting Mexicans." One Texas deputy, Orendáin continues, "bragged that he shot Mexican wets the same way he did rattlesnakes."

Leaving the river, Orendáin and I stop at a cafe for coffee. In a newspaper we read an Associated Press report:

"Tiburcio Griego Santome of Juárez, Mexico, was shot to death in the car of Glasscock County Sheriff Royce Pruitt by a retired West Texas deputy. Santome was dead on arrival at a Big Spring clinic." The story adds that Texas Rangers were called in to investigate the shooting death of the Mexican.

"Another case of the police investigating the police," Orendáin comments. "And meanwhile another Mexican is dead. You will never hear *his* side of the story."

Later we read in another newspaper that two former Houston policemen were indicted for murder in the death of a Mexican American. They were accused of beating the 23-year-old man and pushing him off a 16-foot embankment into a downtown bayou. An all-white jury convicted them of the lesser crime of criminally negligent homicide.

"This has a penalty of no more than a year in jail," Orendáin remarks, "but a lesser sentence, with time off for good behavior, could cut the time they actually serve to a few months, if anything."

My goal remains before me: to become a wetback for a moment in time, to try to understand the dangers he faces, the life of fear he leads.

I stay for a while in the home of Teresa Tijerina in McAllen, north of Hidalgo in Texas. She is a sister of Raul Yzaguirre, a friend who heads the National Council of La Raza, an organization working for Hispanic rights.

One day one of Teresa's children, nine-year-old Adriana Estela, with whom I share a bedroom asks:

"If you had your choice to go anywhere in the world, where would you go?"

I am lucky, I tell her. I have that choice. And I have been lots of places.

"Hong Kong . . . and France?" she asks.

Yes.

"And now where would you most like to go?"

I want to swim the Rio Grande, I tell her. And I realize that you sometimes tell a child what you can't tell an adult. I prefer being here to being on the Aegean, the Nile, or the Mediterranean .. to anywhere on earth. It is my choice. I have traveled enough to feel a great liberation—places no longer are important. Only people.

I know one day I *will* cross because it is what I want most to do. For me this is what living means: a chance to listen to my inner voice, to do what I want to do, to increase knowledge, to strive for understanding. And it is for my understanding that I want to "pass" as a wetback. I know that no person born with white skin can know the discrimination that a person born with color suffers in white America. But I can *try* to know. And I can know, to some extent. Already, I have begun to question: Why am I legal and millions of others illegal? It is human to have a dream and try to fulfill it.

Eventually I confide in Teresa, and in Teresa's mother, Eva. Teresa drives me across the river, to Reynosa in Mexico, where we talk with her cousin's husband, a large, impressive Mexican with a Pancho Villa mustache. He says, "No problem." He will contact illegals who swim over regularly and I can go without papers as one of them. We think it is all arranged. But the next day Teresa's cousin calls to say her husband was called away "on an emergency."

Teresa thinks of a Mexican friend, Noe O'Cana, who lives in Reynosa and who has bragged about the times as a youngster he swam the Rio Grande. Each Saturday he'd take fruit from Mexico, sell it in Texas, and go to the movies. But when we visit him he says he has "forgotten" how to swim. Then sheepishly he admits he's grown older and "more afraid" of the river. Teresa next recalls a Mexican, Adolfo Trujillo, who once did construction work for her. He too lives in Reynosa, but crosses illegally by the river. We drive to Reynosa's worst barrio, the streets a series of small arroyos filled with foul-smelling, mosquito-breeding puddles. The houses are stitched together pieces of tin and cardboard. Inside one hovel, I meet Isidra Trujillo, prominently pregnant, her seven children, and her husband, a handsome man of 44, from San Miguel de Allende in Guanajuato. He's working on the Mexican side now, he tells us. He stopped swimming the river after he saw two dead men floating alongside him.

Had the men been shot? Had they drowned?

Trujillo shrugged. He did not know.

The next morning, back in Texas, Teresa brings in the McAllen *Monitor*. We read on the front page: "Another body was recovered from the Rio Grande Saturday, according to Hidalgo County Deputy Sheriff Gus Sánchez. The body of a Mexican youth, about 5 feet, 7 inches tall, weight 160 pounds, was found near the banks of the river east of Hidalgo. There was no identification, tattoos or other marks on the body, which the deputy estimated had been in the water three or four days. The Justice of the Peace ruled accidental drowning."

Teresa does not believe the Mexican drowned accidentally. "I've read too many stories like that. A Mexican can swim that river—and you can swim it. The danger is getting shot when you get to shore."

Eventually I decide I must go alone to the Central Plaza in Reynosa, Mexico, where I have been told Mexicans planning a crossing gather. They come from the interior of Mexico by bus, and go immediately to the plaza. There they talk freely of their planned crossings. They do not fear Mexican police. For Mexico, the poor jobless who leave provide a safety valve to their depressed economy.

I sit on a park bench and nod affirmatively when a six-year-old shoe-shine boy solicits a job. I watch as he takes a brown bottle from a cigar box and begins polishing my old loafers. His name, he says, is Jesús, and he wants to practice his English: "You happy? Me very happy." Jesús is one of the lucky ones in Mexico: He has some money in his pocket. At this moment he is not starving.

Nowhere else on the globe do two nations representing such disparate worlds confront each other so directly as

Mexico and the United States. Nowhere else in the world
are so many people—wildly hungry for jobs and food—
forced to live so close to so many of the super rich.

The jobless, hungry Mexicans milling around me have
their minds and hearts fixed across a river. They visualize
a land that offers more hope and the promise of a better
life than any other country in the world. And they are
right. Sitting in the Reynosa plaza, I overhear two men
talking about a crossing. One says he's not well, he can't
go. My eyes concentrate on the other: Husky, not fat.
About five feet, eight. Mid-twenties. Serious face. Indian
features, with aquiline nose, high cheekbones, and abundant, straight, black hair. I instinctively accept him as a
friend. Sometimes we think that to go into a strange
world we must know influential people and friends of
friends. But for me, it has been the stranger casually
encountered who most often has proven to be my brother,
my friend.

The other man is leaving when I approach. Nodding
toward the river, I ask my "friend" in Spanish: Is it
difficult?

"You want to cross?"

Yes.

"To get a job—or something?"

Something, I say. I drop my head in silence. Perhaps
my silence and bowed head lead him to believe I have
committed a serious crime and must escape quickly. If so,
he will not be my judge:

"Your *past*," he tells me, "is not important." He is a
simple man who sees me as he sees himself, a vulnerable,
defenseless person. He accepts me as the poor of this
world always seem to accept another: on face value. Just
as he knows he will be classified as "criminal" for swimming the river, he sees me as one who like himself can not
qualify for documents—for one of a thousand reasons.

"If you don't have papers," he almost whispers, "that is
your business."

We have begun to move out of the plaza, unconsciously assuming a conspiratorial tone: "Another person drowned yesterday," he says in a low voice.

We walk north, two persons among a milling throng, coming to know one another, curious about our dreams. I learn his name is César Guerrero Paz, and he was born in a remote village in the state of Michoacán, in the northwest plateau, one of Mexico's most beautiful states but also one of its poorest. Land farmed for centuries has become depleted of minerals. Fertilizers and farm implements often cost too much for the peasants. Farmers, who can't rely on sufficent rain, attempt to raise corn and beans.

More than 75 percent of all Mexican illegals, a government survey showed, come from Michoacán and nine other plateau and border states. A man like Guerrero cannot make a living in these states. His village is like others where I have lived: There is no electricity and when the sun goes down you have only a flickering candle or a kerosene lamp between you and the darkness. There is one telephone—but his family never has spoken on it. There is a one-room school, but most of the people—his parents among them—never had the opportunity to attend class. Guerrero went to the school "off and on" long enough to learn to write his name, which is a proud accomplishment to him. But he had no opportunities for advancement in life. The land which he and his family worked for a boss or *patrón* would never be their land.

Older men in Guerrero's village frequently went to and from *el norte*. The ritual of their departures and their homecomings was as much a part of village life as the baptism of babies, the celebration of weddings, and going to vespers. His mother's brother went as a contract laborer under the bracero program and returned to Mexico with a small, battery-operated radio that he gave to Guerrero. The boy would cup it against his ear, listening to the Voice of America that out of the nothingness of space spoke to him in Spanish, telling him of a land where people championed Human Rights and gave everyone a chance. The Voice seemed to tell Guerrero: Come to this land.

He was 18 when his father died and his mother looked to him, as the oldest of her eight children, to become head of the family. Guerrero headed north. He hitched rides on trucks to Reynosa, went to the Central Plaza—where we had met—and encountered two other youths. They swam the river together, then parted—to go separate ways. Guerrero worked at various jobs for a year, never being detected and sending home most of what he earned. But after a year, hearing through a friend that his mother was ill, he went home to see her. He was with her for two weeks, "and then she died." Now he has come north again to work. His two younger brothers work in the fields and he is the sole support for his four sisters. He speaks fondly of his sisters, relating their names and ages.

Help me, I ask Guerrero, as he would a sister. I know he plans to cross. And I want to go when he does.

He warns of the dangers: snakes, wild animals, thorny cactus, and brush. "Everything you touch scratches, tears, bites, or is poisonous." Then you face armed agents of the Immigration and Naturalization Service—*la migra,* as Guerrero calls them. "They are all along the river. They have seeing devices. They talk to each other on radios. And they have aircraft overhead." He speaks as though we are two small people going against an army of trained men with the world's most sophisticated weapons. And we are. Besides *la migra,* we face rifle-carrying Texas farmers and ranchers, city policemen and sheriffs' deputies, as well as armed vigilantes who will shoot anyone who is brown and throw him in the river.

Women, Guerrero adds, are especially vulnerable. "There are men all along the river who assault and rape the women they catch coming in."

He waits for me to say I've changed my mind. He takes my silence to mean I still want to cross. Then he says it's the same with him; he has no other choice.

We discuss the crossing. He thinks we could use an innertube and swim across with less splashing. Splashing too much, he warns, is the same as calling to *la migra*. I walk with him to several homes in the same barrio where I had visited the Trujillo family with Teresa Tijerina. He finds an innertube which is no more than a collection of patches held together by a bit of rubber. It will not hold air.

It is after nine in the evening now, and very dark. Guerrero advises against crossing this late. Since he has assumed the role of a "brother," I acquiesce. He suggests *mañana*, in the evening. He points out a particular sagebush and says he'll meet me there. Six-thirty is a good time, about dusk, he adds. This will be the time when visibility will be poorest. Before *la migra* can effectively use their night-seeing telescopes, and track us down.

The next evening, before leaving Texas, I ask Teresa: Does she think he will be there?

"Yes, if he doesn't have anything better to do."

His suggesting *mañana* might be an easy way of his keeping face, while losing me. But I have implicit faith in him. I need this trust, this faith in another. I use it like a crutch. I am going to a "foreign" country with none of my possessions save my shoes, shorts, and a halter underneath an old dress Teresa has loaned to me, together with a small purse and a few coins. I leave behind all proof that I am a United States citizen. I have no passport, credit cards, Social Security card, or driver's license. I feel vulnerable, unsure I can return to security.

From McAllen, I take a bus over a bridge into Mexico. No policeman boards the bus to check papers. It is easy to go to Mexico without papers, but difficult to enter the

United States without documents. Sitting at the back of the bus, surrounded by Mexicans, I recall the words of Teresa's mother: that she would pray for me. I need the power of her prayers. It is a mystery which I accept and which no one can explain.

In downtown Reynosa, Mexico, I get off the bus. I walk toward the river and along the levee. Half hidden behind a sage bush, I see Guerrero's Indian face with his abundant black hair combed straight back.

He greets me with a nod. I reach to touch his hand to convey my pleasure in his presence. Intuitively I have accepted my knowing him as a friend, without knowing why.

Guerrero still has not found a suitable innertube. "We will cross without it," he says, again reminding me not to splash while swimming.

We walk to the river.

I feel a heightened awareness of the beauty of this earth. The sun has set, but its dying rays etch pink fringes around blue-white clouds. Water that had looked muddy now glistens—I see a million silvery coins dancing on the waves. So perfect is our understanding that I now can talk to this man beside me without words. You, César Guerrero Paz, whose history I barely know, whose future I can not know—you and I have this moment, a sharing. I want to cling to you, to keep you forever in my life, but let it be. This moment is all, for me, for us.

At the riverbank, he removes shoes, trousers.

I take off my shoes, put them and the old dress I borrowed from Teresa into a plastic bag. I am down to my shorts and halter.

Guerrero takes both his and my plastic bags and together we wade into the Rio Grande. I imagine Border Patrolmen on the Texas shore, their binoculars trained on us. I have a fear that angry, armed men will kill me before I can shout, Wait! I am innocent. And I know that

almost any Mexican who has been shot could have
shouted, and perhaps did shout. Yet he was shot anyway.

I try to concentrate only on the moment. We stand
ankle-deep in the water, and Guerrero—to dispel my
fears—reminds me that in crossing it is not so important
to be a good swimmer but to have confidence, be sure of
yourself. "Many drown," he says, "because they panic
when they meet an unexpectedly swift current or treach-
erous eddy."

The water beats with whirlpool force about my body.
I'm waist deep—then I feel my feet swept off the sand. I
begin to swim, splashing noisily, frantically slapping legs
and arms against the water to keep up, the way I learned
in Texas creeks. I see Guerrero propelling himself for-
ward with strong, silent strokes. He shortens his distance, swims beside me: "I am here, *estoy aquí*," he
reminds me. His reassuring words release my fears. Now
I lengthen my strokes, making every motion surer,
smoother, swifter. Once I try to look at the shore to see if
armed guards are waiting to arrest us. As I look for *la
migra*, I forget my breathing, water runs into my mouth,
and I start coughing loudly. Guerrero whispers to me to
be silent. I try to put *la migra* out of mind. I concentrate
on my breathing and a face of one I love. This love
supports me, as does Guerrero, swimming beside me.

We reach the shoreline, and we wade into the Promised
Land.

Guerrero hands me my plastic bag. Each of us goes into
the brush. We remove our wet clothes and put on the dry
ones.

Together we climb the steep embankment. Silently, we
pause for breath trying to prepare ourselves against a
sudden attack. All is jungle quiet. The buzz of an insect
seems amplified. We come to a clearing.

"Listen!" Guerrero whispers. We hear the drone of a
plane, and fall to the ground like soldiers in an attack.

"Here—hide!" Guerrero commands, pulling me after him into a shelter of thorny bushes. I am scratched and bleeding, but do not immediately notice. This, I know, is not foreign soil to Guerrero. Like his Indian ancestors, he knows how to hide in scrub, oleander, sage, mesquite. We barely breathe, listening to the plane overhead.

Like any "fugitive" I do not want to find myself behind bars, denied the right to see the sky, reduced to a numbered object, easily lost in a maze of statistics, my whereabouts a mystery to family and friends.

I recall Teresa's mother saying, "Aren't you afraid of being shot?"

Of course I am afraid. But if life ends, I will have been one of the lucky ones. And if there is another day, that will be a bonus.

We stay motionless, silent in the bushes. The drone of the plane diminishes.

We each breathe a sigh of relief. Psychologically we have crossed the "greatest of all rivers," for the Rio Grande to Mexicans is like Dante's allegorical River Styx—it separates Hell from Heaven-on-Earth.

But even in this Paradise, Guerrero will forever be halfway in Hell. I think of his future life. He and I are still hiding, but he will always have to hide, a fugitive from justice, subject to every abuse. I try to imagine the loneliness Guerrero suffers being in a land whose cultural and social values are foreign to him. He does not speak the language, he is hundreds of miles from his loved ones. Guerrero cannot write to his family, and his family cannot write to him, for they do not know how.

Guerrero suggests we remain hidden in the bushes for half an hour. If we have triggered sensor devices in *la migra* headquarters in McAllen, agents in scout cars will be speeding to an area a fast-moving wetback would reach after 30 minutes travel. But by remaining hidden we will not be in that area. "They'll think a jack rabbit has triggered the sensor, and they'll leave," Guerrero explains.

I ask Guerrero how he knows so much about *la migra* and their sophisticated weapons. He says the wetbacks in the Reynosa plaza and in their home villages talk endlessly about the tactics of *la migra*. "Our lives depend on our knowing," he adds.

What will he do now—does he think he can find work?

"There's plenty of work in this country," he says. It is highly relevant that men such as Guerrero do find work even when the United States unemployment rate in some states stands at seven to eight percent. This suggests that men such as Guerrero are not taking jobs away from Americans, but rather are prepared to do menial jobs that even jobless Americans will not accept.

On his first trip, he mopped floors, mowed grass, worked in a packing plant, ran an elevator. I look anew at his Indian face, his dark skin, and realize he is un-schooled, with no special skills. Guerrero tells me: "My honor comes not from my job, but how well I do that job." He adds, "My bosses have all liked my work."

Guerrero's last job was as a dishwasher in a Dallas restaurant where he earned $1.10 an hour. He plans to return there and, if *la migra* doesn't catch him, hopes his former boss will be glad to see him.

We have agreed that once we start walking we will go in different directions—it will be easier for us to hide. I walk toward safety and friends. But he faces an unknown future with nothing more than his courage to sustain him.

III

Life on the Border

All along the border—from Brownsville to San Diego—I stayed with families who live and have relatives in both the United States and Mexico. As they tell their stories, they or their forebears have always been in this land. The migration of their Indian ancestors from north to south began some thirty thousand years ago and going north again is as natural to them as it is for birds, animals, or the wind.

We may brand César Guerrero Paz, the wetback with whom I swam the Rio Grande, as a newcomer, an interloper, an illegal, but actually he comes from the longest line of legals we have in this country. His Indian forebears—and Mexicans such as Guerrero are for the most part Indian—were the native Americans; and his Spanish-speaking forebears were the second oldest of the legals—the Spaniards being the first Europeans to bring

western civilization to this New World. Beginning four
hundred years ago, the Spaniards discovered, charted,
and traveled trails north from Mexico. For more than a
century now Mexicans such as Guerrero have moved in
the millions back and forth over those same trails, many
of them now rail lines and highways. In such a historical
setting, the word "illegal" has only the meaning that we
ourselves give it.

I stayed with various families in the borderlands, an
area that includes parts of four of our states and six
Mexican states. Throughout this area, on both sides of
the border, I could sense a spirit of place. I could feel the
years under my feet. This area that was once a part of
Mexico is still new to the Anglos. It comprises some of
our newest states and it is the fastest growing part of our
country. Yet it, along with Florida, has the oldest written
history in the United States.

The history of the Southwest was written by the
ancestors of the Mexicans—the Indians and the Spaniards. In talking with Mexican Americans I asked them
why they felt themselves different from Anglo Americans—and by Anglos I mean all of us (including blacks)
who are not Hispanos.

"Our long history in this country makes us different,"
Elisa Rodriguez, a Catholic nun in El Paso, told me.
Saying she could trace her family tree back more than
three hundred years in America, she explained that the
King of Spain had given her family a land grant in 1670,
and that this land remained in her family until Anglos
moved into the area and took possession.

Sister Elisa and I often walked along the streets of El
Paso, near the Port of Entry, where we saw signs only in
Spanish, heard only Spanish spoken, and—for the most
part—saw only Mexican people. I quickly forgot that I
was in the United States. And for a good reason: Spanish
was the principal language of El Paso for over three

hundred years. Even as recently as 1877 there were twelve thousand people living in El Paso, all but 80 of whom were Mexicans.

The history of the city goes back much further. The site was first visited by Spaniards more than two decades before the Pilgrims landed at Plymouth, and it has been Spanish and Mexican far longer than it has been part of the United States. In 1598 a party of Spaniards, commanded by Captain General Don Juan de Oñate, sighted a river that cut a pass between two mountains. In finding the Rio Grande and the pass, the Spaniards broke a new trail from Mexico City to Spain's New Mexican kingdom. The Spaniards named the site The Pass to the North, *El Paso del Norte.*

In recounting this history, Sister Elisa said most Anglos did not understand that the Spaniards brought so much to this New World. "They brought the wheel to this country. They brought the first cattle, horses, goats, pigs, barnyard fowls. The Indians had only wild turkeys. The Spaniards also brought the first hoes and spades and agricultural tools. They began our system of irrigation. They planted the first wheat, sugar cane, cotton." She also pointed out that the Spaniards solved the problem of building without timber by using mud-and-straw adobe, and created a style of architecture that can be seen throughout the Southwest today. Moreover, many of the adobe missions the Spaniards built nearly four hundred years ago are still standing.

Another Catholic Sister, Yolanda Taronga, stressed that the heritage bequeathed by the Spaniards extended throughout the United States. "The Spaniards named more than two thousand cities and towns in the United States—more than four hundred of these in California, two hundred and fifty in Texas and New Mexico, and more than one hundred in Colorado and Arizona," she told me. She added that Spanish place names appear in

every state of the Union. A vivacious, attractive woman
in her 30s, Sister Yolanda showed me her family home in
the El Paso suburb of Ysleta, the oldest settlement in the
Southwest. Together we visited the Ysleta mission built
by the Spaniards in 1682.

"I can trace my roots here back for seven generations,"
she told me. "My grandmother and my father and I all
went to the same school. We have a great sense of
belonging here."

From El Paso I traveled to a small town in New Mexico
called Las Vegas, meaning "The Meadows," to visit two
old settlers whose names had been given me by their
nephew, Pablo Sedillo, in Washington, D. C. Sedillo, who
can trace his family history back 12 generations, assured
me I would get a sense of Indian-Spanish-Mexican
history by visiting his uncles.

I knocked on the door of a small, stucco house, with
honeysuckle, snapdragons, and hollyhocks out front. It
was midmorning. The brothers Cruz and Zacarías Sedillo
welcomed me and, as we sat around a kitchen table,
Zacarías prepared cups of tea from herbs he had plucked
from the fields. The brothers, born in 1891 and 1902, enjoy
enormous vitality. Their hearing is good and so also their
eyesight. Neither uses glasses and their blue eyes sparkle
as they talk. They have amazing memories for dates,
places, and events. As they talked I pieced together a
fabric of their history: In the late 1500s when the first
Sedillos came from Spain, New Mexico was largely a
virgin land of untrammeled fields, a peaceful Garden of
Eden save for skirmishes with nomadic Indian tribes who
outnumbered the Spaniards more than ten to one.

The early Sedillos banded together with other settlers
in a series of outer defenses in mountain villages such as
Cundiyo, Cordova, Truchas, Las Trampas, Chamisal,
Peñasco. These settlements, dating from the late 1500s
and among the oldest in the United States, are a century

older than those in Texas and two centuries older than those of California. The Spaniards founded Santa Fe (Holy Faith), the oldest capital in the United States, in 1609.

Although only a few in number—no more than three to four thousand in the seventeenth and eighteenth centuries—the Spaniards neverthless maintained strength because of their cohesiveness.

"This town once was a resting place for the caravans coming up from Mexico," Zacarías related. "They'd rest here before going on through the canyons on their way to Santa Fe. In the early years, New Mexico was almost completely isolated. It took five months to make the 1,200 mile round trip along the Turquoise Trail from Chihuahua to Santa Fe. If you lived in Santa Fe and had a problem, you'd write your boss in Mexico City. But it would take a couple of years for you to get an answer."

The Sedillos explained that they got their language and religion from their Spanish forebears, and that Indian ancestors bequeathed a knowledge of hunting, farming, and a devout reverence for the land.

"In the olden days, food was always on the trees, in the ground, and hanging out drying," Cruz continued. "We worked hard. We were healthy. We were out in the open, from early morning to night, working in the fields. We didn't know anything about high blood pressure, cancer, TB, or heart attacks."

Both brothers stressed repeatedly during my visit that their long history in this country gave them a sense of being different from the later arrivals, the Anglo Americans. Zacarías joked about this, saying "We Hispanos were here so long we were forgotten." Now, however, with the illegals in the news, "We're being rediscovered."

I drove over much of New Mexico with Roberto Salazar, a historian and a native of Española, northwest of Santa Fe. Once we were leaving Albuquerque and I could see the Rio Grande in the distance.

"Coronado was here in 1540. In 1940 we held a four hundredth anniversary of his visit," Salazar related. "The Spanish-Mexican Southwest is more than twice the age of the rest of the United States that, in 1976, celebrated its bicentennial."

I gleaned a sense of history also from the Tijerina and Yzaguirre families in McAllen, when I stayed in the home of Teresa Tijerina. Teresa once said: "For me, what makes us different from the Anglos is the strength of our families." Teresa, in emphasizing the family, was echoing from her personal experience what the anthropologist Margaret Mead had observed: "to be Hispanic is to be a member of a family." There's another distinction in the case of Teresa and others like her who live along the border: They are members of a family living in two distinct worlds, both equally important to them. Teresa's family moves back and forth across the border by day and by night, speaking English or Spanish or both, at ease with the Anglo manners of Texas while cherishing countless old Spanish and Mexican traditions.

Teresa, 32, attractive, and the mother of five, is a citizen of the United States. She introduces me to her mother-in-law, a neighbor, who gave birth to eight children, seven of them born in the United States and United States citizens. The one Teresa married, Manuel, was born in Mexico, and remains a citizen of Mexico. "He has a passport and can come and go as he pleases." She adds that Manuel does not wish to become a United States citizen.

Teresa and I visit her parents, Ruben and Eva Yzaguirre, who live nearby. Ruben Yzaguirre, in his seventies, an expansive man in girth and spirit, recalls he was four years old when poor Mexican peasants began their revolution to wrest land from the rich. In that year, 1910, a fifth of Mexico—about one hundred and fifty thousand square miles, or an area larger than Italy or Japan—was owned by 17 families. Ninety-six percent of the population owned only 1 percent of the land, while 1 percent owned 97 percent. Yzaguirre's family was among the 1 percent that owned 97 percent. His family was so rich "they had fringes of gold on their bedspreads and curtains."

In the revolution, they lost all their vast holdings. "But, it was right to break up the big holdings and make a more equitable distribution of the land with the poor," Yzaguirre believes.

The uprisings against the rich ended in 1917 with a constitution guaranteeing the redistribution of the large estates. Land ownership was restricted by law to no more than 250 acres. It is a good law, but one Mexico has not enforced.

"At the time of the revolution, some of my brothers and sisters stayed in Mexico and some in Texas," Yzaguirre continues. When he was a child his mother was ill, and he was raised by his father's sister. "My real mother was in Ciudad Camargo in Mexico, and my aunt was in Rio Grande in Texas. I called them both 'mama.' When I was eight I'd go down on the river—just a kid, alone—and get the boat from Rio Grande to Camargo. The boatman always asked, 'Where you going, son?' and I'd say, 'To see my mama.' And when I'd be returning to Camargo he'd ask, 'Now, where you going, son?' and I'd say, 'To see my mama.' "

Eva Yzaguirre recalls that her parents, who were both from Monterrey in Mexico, told her that immediately after they were married they left for Texas. Later they visited in Monterrey and upon returning to the border had to fill out forms and get a pass. "That was in 1924. My mother said it was the first year you were required to show any documents."

The Yzaguirres introduce me to numerous friends who tell similar stories of crossing without papers. "I came here with my parents in 1916 soon after the revolution,"

Julia López Puente relates. She adds that she has a son at
Fort Bliss near El Paso who has served 22 years in the
United States Army.

Then, I ask, is she a United States citizen?

"No," she replies in Spanish. "I have never become a
citizen because I don't know enough English. Also, I like
to retain my ties to Mexico. I feel I belong to both
countries." As in fact she does.

Once Teresa and I lunched with several old-timers,
friends of her parents. One, Ireneo Sanchez Espinoza,
born in 1904, showed me a United States residence card,
dated January 8, 1916. "I came during the revolution in
1915," he related. "My mother, father, the whole family,
came over by boat. There wasn't any charge." Another,
Basilio Castillo, 90, tells me he came over for one reason:
"to work." He got a job in the San Juan water department "and I worked there for 57 years." He first crossed
to *el norte* from his home state of San Luis Potosí in 1912:
"Anyone from Mexico could come and go as you pleased
in those years. It was the same as being in one country."

At the luncheon with the old people I noticed the
tenderness Teresa extended to the friends of her parents.
She called several by endearing names such as "my dear
aunt," or "my dear uncle"—and it sounded natural and
right in Spanish, even though they were not related to
her. She pointed out that millions of Anglos are old and
neglected, "but in our family we will never allow this to
happen." No one, she said firmly, should be old—and
alone.

Having said this, Teresa recalls to mind her father's
sister Delia who lives alone. "We should visit her." And
over the following days an outing to the ranch in Mexico
is planned. Although, "planned" is not quite the word.
With Latinos a program is not so much "planned" as
allowed to unfold as nature or *Dios* or fate intends. This
means that one is so busy dealing with the confusion of

the present that the future must take care of itself.

Early one Sunday morning, Ruben and Eva Yzaguirre arrive with a daughter-in-law and baskets of edibles, ready to leave for Mexico.

Manuel Tijerina is packing for another trip to Mexico City, although he will first drive us to the house of Delia's daughter, Elia Garza de la Garza, across the border in Reynosa.

Manuel puts his suitcase and garment bag in the car. Then we all bemoan the fact that Teresa cannot go with us. Tina, the baby sitter, is here with her sister, Elidora-Dulcinea, but it's really Tina's day off and the girls are waiting for boyfriends coming in by bus from Rio Bravo in Mexico to take them out for the day.

Eleven-year-old Marla says, "I'll stay, mama."

"No, dear," says her mother, "I'm not going to deprive you of this pleasure." With that, Marla dashes down the street in search of a neighbor to watch the children.

Meanwhile Manuel has started the motor. He and Ruben Yzaguirre sit in the car, and Manuel blares the horn for us to hurry. Marla returns with a baby sitter, Teresa gets her purse, and we all pile into two cars and start for the home of Aunt Delia's daughter in Reynosa.

The Mexican border guards wave us through the Port of Entry at Hidalgo-Reynosa. And we're in Mexico.

By noon we are at the home of Delia's daughter, Elia. Manuel bids us goodbye, and leaves in his car for Mexico City. Teresa says she should have brought some food for Aunt Delia, so she and I and one of Elia's daughters walk to a neighborhood market and buy mangoes, oranges, and tomatoes. Lalo, Elia's husband, meanwhile has gone in his pickup truck to buy ice.

Eventually 15 of us and two dogs pack ourselves into Lalo's pickup truck—Lalo, Elia, Teresa, and Eva in the cab. I suggest Ruben Yzaguirre, who is over 70 and recently suffered a stroke, should be up front. But he won't hear of it.

We take off hurriedly, then stop to buy a hat for Elia. Then again we're off—and again we stop, this time to buy tortillas.

Eventually we clip along at a steady speed down a two-lane highway due south. After an hour Lalo turns onto a dirt road.

"The ranch starts here," Yzaguirre tells me. I see little grass, lots of cacti and mesquite, a variety of cattle: the white French Charolais, and a mixture of white-faced Hereford with a native cattle called *criolla*. We approach a small, unpainted, frame house set in a landscape of arid sand and mesquite.

Aunt Delia, a large woman who resembles her brother, Ruben, greets us amid great rejoicing.

We all sit on a small front porch, and the oppressively hot Sunday afternoon evolves in slow motion. Chickens half-heartedly peck at our feet and at a large watermelon rolled in a corner. Elisa serves us a cool, sweet, purplish drink made from Jamaica flowers. The scene takes me back to hot, summer, childhood days in Texas. A visitor, a breeze, or a cool, tall drink was cause for celebration. We had no air conditioning, no TV. We passed the time in talk. As does Teresa's family.

"I'm strong as a mule, but mother was delicate," Delia relates. "We had moved back to Mexico from Texas, and the Mexicans arrested my father because he had a cousin who was a colonel in the revolution. Mother was pregnant, and seeing the soldiers arrest my father and take him to jail she got ill. She lost the baby. I remember her crying—and crying." Delia herself begins to cry. Eva and Teresa comfort her, as if they were hearing the story for the first time.

Meanwhile, Lalo has killed a goat, and he and Elia

prepare it three different ways: They grill the ribs, they steam the intestines with a hot sauce, and they fry the remaining sections, adding as a relish the blood of the goat. An animal's blood, they say, gives strength.

Delia and Elia, serving us in a small room extending from the kitchen, hover around the table, anxious to be sure we have everything we need. In addition to the three varieties of goat meat, we eat rice with onions, tamales, and a macaroni-mayonnaise salad. Despite the heat, we all eat heartily.

After lunch, the men disappear outdoors to talk. And the women gather in Delia's bedroom, shoes off and half undressed, to discuss our lives. It is a long afternoon, with endless talk. Nothing much happened, and this perhaps is the whole point: The strength of the Mexican family may lie in their simply taking the time to listen to each other talk.

The people with whom I visited—the Catholic nuns and priests, the brothers Sedillo, Teresa Tijerina—all think of the states along the border of Mexico and the United States as united. The borderlands constitute a binational, bicultural, bilingual regional entity, a zone of interlocking economic, social, and cultural interests. There is nothing like this symbiotic relationship along any other border of comparable length in the world.

A dozen bridges spanning the Rio Grande link the two countries. Fourteen railway lines, all of them carrying freight—much of which passes "in bond," without inspection by customs—connect these areas. Business is booming. For instance, as many as three hundred trucks a day enter Nogales, Arizona, carrying more than a billion pounds of vegetables each year that are then transshipped to other markets. New highways stimulate trade and tourism.

The annual border crossings indicate the magnitude of the exchange and contacts that now take place: they total more than two hundred million people a year through 24 Ports of Entry.

Mexicans cross to the United States to buy TVs, radios, clothes, canned goods. They give most United States border towns half or more of their income. Meanwhile, Americans—both brown and Anglo—cross from the United States into Mexico to visit dentists, beauticians, barbers, all of whom charge less than half American prices. Also they buy fruits and vegetables in Mexico. They usually are fresher and tastier, and always cheaper than on the United States side. Mexican Americans go across the border to meet relatives and friends with whom they observe the same religious rites and celebrate the same festivals. They go to bull fights, cock fights, soccer games. They share common passions and delights: a love for romance, the stability of a friendship, gaiety, music, dance and good food. The Americans enjoy Mexican music, handicrafts, and cooking. Until recently, however, only a few have probed deeper, to study the culture, language, and philosophy.

The border area, once dubbed the cactus country until irrigation made the desert bloom, has the same soil, produces the same fruits and vegetables, and has the same problems. It is chronically short of water. It is plagued by the rapid growth of cities. Seen in this light, Mexico is not "foreign" as England or Japan might be, but an extension of our Southwest. Or, to put it another way, our Southwest has remained a part of Mexico.

"The Spanish-speaking people have a way of surviving," Roberto Salazar of Albuquerque told me. "And something interesting, even historical, is happening out here today. You know the United States defeated Mexico and took the Southwest. Now I really think we are in the midst of a new conquest type of thing, and we have been for many decades. In any conquest the conquerors somehow are conquered to a certain degree. It's like the Nile river that overflows its banks—it carries something of the banks with it. The conquering Anglo culture in this case has been and will be influenced more than it wants to be, more than it is aware of." He points out that increasing numbers of Anglos and Mexicans are moving into the fastest growing section of the United States, and that "the final victory" to determine who controls the land is still somewhat in doubt.

IV

With Women to the Promised Land

One Monday morning, I am in Juárez, Mexico, across the border from El Paso, Texas, staying with María and Diego Montoya. Diego has left for his job and María prepares me a cup of herbal tea, assuring me with her nurturing gesture that I am not entirely alone. Again, I have none of my papers, credentials, or identification cards here in Mexico. Only my clothes—old shoes, slacks, and a shirt. And a purse with a few coins. Like millions of others, I have no way to prove that I am legal.

Two months earlier, almost a thousand miles downstream, I swam across the Rio Grande with an illegal, César Guerrero Paz, to better understand his life as a wetback. Now I want to cross with a Mexican woman, to understand, if possible, something about her life, what motivates her to leave home and family, to risk insults, imprisonment, assault, rape, even life itself, to reach a land that for her spells hope and a new beginning.

Formerly, only undocumented Mexican men came to the States. They left their wives and children back home. They had to do so. They were often without jobs or food. When they worked, they sent money to their families back home. Now, however, women no longer feel chained to a home or children. They come over as single or married women. If they have children, they leave them with a relative or a friend. Like men, they come to get any work they can find.

Mexican women represent one third of all the illegals being apprehended in the large cities such as New York. The women behind bars, arrested for crossing without papers, tell the same stories: "I want to work. I want to earn the kind of money I could never earn in Mexico." Immigration officials have difficulty adjusting to these changes. Formerly, they say, if they arrested a female, they expected her to be a prostitute. When I ask about the biggest changes they have seen in the past few years, they all said: the increase in the number of women who are coming over. "Before, we never saw women," veteran Agent Harold Williamson of El Paso told me. Now, he added, almost every group that moves has perhaps one third to one half women.

Most of the illegal women cross from Juárez to its twin city, El Paso, because it is fairly easy to cross there. At Juárez–El Paso, the Rio Grande makes a slow turn from south to east. In this turn, the Great River diminishes to a sluggish stream, so shallow that one can often wade or walk across. The illegals joke about this, saying that on some days if you want to be a wetback, "you have to carry your own water."

María Montoya, a sturdily built woman with Indian features, with whom I am staying, says that before she got a card that permits her to walk across the Juárez–El Paso bridge into the United States, she often crossed the Rio Grande illegally. She did not swim, she did not wade, but rather rode piggyback style on the shoulders of a strong Mexican.

She describes the "local ferry" service for illegal women:

"Usually you can find such a man along the river. He puts you on his shoulders. You hold your feet up near his chest. Your clothes will not get wet. He walks across and deposits you on the United States side. You tip him a few cents. And he goes back for another passenger." Should Border Patrol agents cruise by on the American side of the river, the ferry operation temporarily suspends service.

María says most Mexican women were raised inside the homes, without the opportunities for outdoor sports that Anglo women have. "Most Mexican women, like me, can't swim, and are afraid to go in the river on our own." She believes using the man to carry you over is a neater, more feminine, way of crossing the river than subjecting yourself to the dangers of slipping on stones and arriving at your American employer's door a dripping wetback.

Though women cross illegally for the same reason that the men cross—to get a job in the United States—there is one difference: In almost every case, the men head for the big cities of Detroit, Chicago, Los Angeles, New York, Seattle. The illegal women who cross from Juárez, however, usually are going only as far as El Paso.

There are logical reasons for this. The men have been crossing for generations, and know better where to get good jobs. The women, who only recently started crossing, generally do not want to venture too far too soon. They are still testing the waters of their liberation. Scores still have young children to raise, and they leave them with relatives in Juárez while they cross the river to work in the homes of Anglos in El Paso.

There's still another reason illegal Mexican women can and do remain along the border to a greater extent than

Mexican men—they often work as domestics in United States homes. Border Patrolmen tend to look the other way when they see an illegal domestic. For instance, I once was cruising in a van with a McAllen Border Patrolman and we passed a shack in the country. A young brown-skinned woman with a slender figure came out of the shack.

"We're sure she's wet," the agent told me.

Then why didn't he arrest and deport her?

"Oh," he replied, "she's a maid, she's not doing any harm." Illegal Mexican males take jobs from Americans, he explained, but it's different with Mexican domestics: If they did not do the job, the job would go begging. They will, he added, work for any wage. Subconsciously he was echoing Jacob Riis who found, when he wrote *How the Other Half Lives* about an earlier wave of immigration, that men will not work for less than it costs them to eat, but women will take any wage so long as they can find a man to help them live.

Destitute, unschooled, unskilled Mexican women have few job opportunities. They want to be domestics, but in many instances their hopes turn to nightmares.

"Many women are brought over. They've been promised decent jobs as domestics, then they're turned into prostitutes," McAllen's Chief Border Patrol Agent Tom Ball told me. As an example, he said ten young women who had been brought into this country by a Houston man were arrested at the Border Patrol checkpoint in Falfurrias. "The girls said they were going to work as maids. We had information, however, they were to be put out on the streets as prostitutes."

I met one such woman. She was apprehended in Houston. I flew in a Southwest Airlines plane with Joe Garza of the Port Isabel Detention Center near Harlingen, Texas, to meet her and other illegals who would be booked—and deported. The woman, Narda Simon Heres, 17, who spoke no English and seemed totally innocent of worldly matters, told me on the flight back to Harlingen that she came from a small Mexican village of less than 100 people. A distant uncle recruited her for a job in Houston. He told her she would work as a maid in a fine American home. Then—with tears welling in her eyes—she related that once in Houston he told her she must earn money by sleeping with men he would procure for her.

Garza believed her story. While still in Houston he had called the Mexican consul, Benjamin Arredondo Pérez. Arredondo sent a representative who met our plane, escorted Narda across the border, and gave her a bus ticket back home. Narda may, however, return again to the United States. Since she has no special skills, she will hope to work as a domestic.

A Mexican American, Leonard Anguiano of San Antonio, who has made a study of illegal maids in this country, estimates that perhaps a million or more undocumented Mexican domestics work in American homes. Twelve to twenty thousand illegal Mexican live-in maids work in San Antonio homes, earning $12 to $15 a week.

"They do all the chores, the cleaning, washing, ironing, and they care for the children six days a week. On Sunday, their one free day, they go to mass at the San Francisco Cathedral and in the afternoon they stroll in a circle in a nearby park. Mexican men, many of them also undocumented, stroll in the other direction, and sometimes they chat," Anguiano related. "The women are cooped up for six days, and this stroll in the park is their one bit of recreation and diversion."

Sixty thousand or more illegal domestics work in Los Angeles, and at least twenty thousand illegal maids work in El Paso. He said the Mexican maids gather in the El Paso Central Park. An Anglo woman drives up and stops at the curb. A jobless maid applies for work by walking over and presenting herself to the woman driver. The Anglo may hire her by the hour, day, or week.

I went to the park one day and chatted with one Mexican domestic, Fernanda Jovis, 42, who said she had worked for a lieutenant, stationed at nearby Fort Bliss, and his family until they were transferred to Germany. "The Anglos living in El Paso are very wealthy," she said. I had already ascertained that she had not traveled further than the border, so how would she know?

"Look up and down these streets, all you see are banks," she replied. I did take a look and she was right. Money comes in, undoubtedly, from the Odessa and Midland oilfields, and then, I reflected, El Paso is the only large city between Dallas and Phoenix, a distance of a thousand miles. The big money, however, does not seep down into Fernanda's hands. The lieutenant and his wife paid her only $16 a week. The most an El Paso domestic makes, she said, was about $25 a week.

Employers, however, often praise the energy, disposition, and resourcefulness of the Mexican maid. Donna Laine of El Paso is an example. When her marriage broke up, Donna, a successful executive in an oil supply company, asked her mother to move in. Then her mother became hospitalized and Donna had to find someone to take care of the house and her three children. She found María Montoya, the woman with whom I am staying in Juárez.

"My kids loved her. And she kept the house spotless," Donna told me. "You could eat off the floors. She's a good carpenter, a good gardener who tended the flowers. She never stopped working. At midnight, when I was trying to sleep, María would still be in the kitchen, scrubbing floors. I would say, 'Please María, go to sleep.'"

Her mother grew worse. One leg was swollen double and doctors advised that it be amputated. María told Donna: "Don't let them do it." She proposed Mexican herbs. Donna and her mother were so desperate they told María to try her remedy. She soaked the leg in a brew she made from herbs and the pain subsided. In two days the infection was reduced and the mother recovered. "María worked a miracle, she is a real doctor," Donna told me. With her mother well, Donna Laine no longer needed María as a full-time maid. The two women remain close friends, however, and it was Donna who first drove me to Juárez to meet María.

One enters the Montoya apartment on the second-story level of a cinderblock building in an over-crowded barrio. Once you open the door you are in María's kitchen, facing the family's most prized possession, a gleaming white refrigerator, not only a convenience but also a status symbol for which María and Diego have worked all their lives. Beyond the kitchen, you look into the bedroom where there is a double bed for María and Diego and a single bed for their daughter, Leonora, 15, the only one of their 14 children who lives with them. After several visits, I came to María's apartment to stay awhile. I had suggested, since all their beds were taken, I could sleep on a pallet on the floor and María agreed.

On a Sunday afternoon, despite the 100-degree heat, María is frying chicken, cooking beans (frijoles), potatoes with small green chilies, and preparing a salad with lettuce, carrots, tomatoes, and avocados. She also wants to make a cake to sell at a church social later in the day, and I help her read the recipe on a box of cake mix she bought in an El Paso store.

As we work, she tells me about her first job as a live-in maid in El Paso. The Anglo woman was very good to her. She paid her $25 a week, and gave her the house key when she and her husband, a retired Army colonel, went on vacation. But, María related, "She had a lover, un amante." She admonished María that if her husband asked where she was on certain late afternoons, she was to say she had gone to the beauty shop. But the woman would come in late, tipsy, her hair disheveled. "Obviously," María relates, "she had not been to a beauty shop." After a year the husband caught her with her lover. The lover fled, unharmed, but the husband fired two shots at his wife, grazing her thighs.

María heard the shots and she ran into the room. At that moment the husband fired again, the shot going between the wife's legs. In that second the wife suffered a stroke which left her paralyzed for six months. María and the husband visited her frequently in the hospital, but she never spoke again.

"She would lie there, tears running down her face," María recalls. The day she died, María packed her bag. The husband has called several times wanting her to work for him. After that bad experience, however, María refused to work for any Anglo as a live-in maid. But she crosses the border, using a pass, three days a week to work for different women on an hourly basis.

I ask her where I might meet illegal Mexican women and cross as one of them. "Go to the black bridge," she tells me.

I repeat: black bridge? And she says, "Yes, hundreds cross there every day. It's painted black, so the Mexicans call it *el puente negro*. It's a Southern Pacific Railway bridge, used only for freight."

But, I ask Maria, are there no guards to check your papers?

"No," she replies, "not on this bridge. There are no checkpoints. You just run across."

Would I have trouble finding it?

"No," she reassures me. "*Every* Mexican in Juárez knows the black bridge."

Leaving the Montoya home, I walk along a dusty road to Insurgentes Street. There I take a bus ride, lasting 30 minutes, then change to a second bus. In downtown Juárez, I see from the bus the large *Paseo del Norte* bridge that legal pedestrians and motorists use. I know

that the small railroad bridge must be nearby. On my
way out of the bus, I pause briefly by the driver, bend
close to his ear and whisper: Where is *el puente negro?*

Among the poor Mexicans along the border, there is a
language understood by all those who do not have proper
documents, and this includes the vast majority. The bus
driver may himself be one of those not able to secure a
passport or crossing card.

"See that blue pickup truck?" the bus driver asks.
"Walk there, then turn. . . ." Disembarking passengers
crowd me off the bus. I merge into a throng of workers,
hurrying in every direction. I walk toward the blue
pickup truck, trying to keep my sense of direction.

Should I turn right or left at the pickup truck? I stop
two Mexican men to ask: Where is *el puente negro?* They
know I am saying: I have no papers; I must cross illegally.
They nervously shift their eyes. If they guide me they
can be mistaken for smugglers. They turn away, then one
turns back and suggests: "You have to look a little
harder." Without committing himself he has given me a
hint to keep going in the same direction.

I pass under the *Paseo del Norte* bridge, and see scores
of men sitting beside its abutment in that half-dazed
moment between sleep and wakefulness. One man strug-
gles with his shoes. Another runs his fingers through his
hair. Perhaps they all crossed the border yesterday, were
apprehended and returned to Mexico. Now it's a new day,
and they may try again. They are among the tens of
thousands of men who have moved north from the
interior of Mexico in search of a job to stay alive.
Penniless, they live like animals, sleeping outdoors on the
ground or on a slab of concrete, in the only clothes they
possess.

Passing under the *Paseo del Norte* bridge, now congested with automobiles and pedestrians, I climb an
embankment to the highway, where two Mexicans are

sitting on a concrete retainer wall. I struggle to climb
onto the wall.

One man turns, extends a hand to help me up. He
smiles, and I notice he has nice even teeth. He and his
companion wear clean slacks, with short-sleeved cotton
shirts, open at the neck. Their hands are smooth and
white. They are office workers, a class apart from the
laborers under the bridge who will dig ditches, bend and
stoop over crops, pour concrete, clean abattoirs. Their
dress and demeanor reveal they have some education,
that they know how to read and write. In a land where a
third of the people don't have these skills, they feel
themselves in a higher class. They may have between
them $100. But in Mexico that first $100 makes the
difference.

We mention the weather. It is hot. *Hace calor.* I learn
the name of the young man with the nice teeth beside
me, Roberto. His companion, more taciturn, is Joaquín.

Across the thoroughfare I see *el puente negro,* a narrow
bridge carrying a single track between steel sides. More
than 50 people have gathered, waiting an opportunity to
cross. On the United States side of the bridge we can see
the green sedan of *la migra.* Roberto, Joaquín, and I
don't say: "We want to cross." But it is apparent from our
poised positions that, once *la migra* leaves, we will leap
up and, like the mass of people before us, dash across the
black bridge to the other world.

In studying the bridge, I see that on this side the
Mexicans have placed wooden planks over the rails to
accommodate more standees. The crowd has increased.
Now 60 or 70 stand on the Mexican side. My eyes shift
across the bridge to the United States side guarded by
the Immigration car. One patrolman sits at the wheel.
One armed man is holding a small army of people at bay.

I listen as Roberto and Joaquín describe an incident at
this bridge. Every Mexican in Juárez knows the story

well. I had heard it from María Montoya. A 20-year-old
Mexican, Manuel Flores-Sota, died here. Roberto relates
he has a cousin who was here when it happened. His
cousin told him that "a Border Patrolman threw Flores-
Sota off the bridge and killed him." To protest his death,
three hundred Mexicans, wearing death masks and shouting "Death to the Border Patrol! This country is ours!"
stormed *el puento negro*. They injured a patrolman then
raced back across the bridge to Mexico.

María, who had followed the story carefully, had told
me United States Border Patrolmen denied that any of
them threw Flores-Sota from the bridge. They say he fell.

Sitting, talking with the men, I come to know them
better. They are about the same age, late twenties, but
one, Joaquín, seems older. They are somehow related, "to
his uncle," Roberto explains, "but through my aunt ..."
and he traces a chain of family connections that boggles
the mind.

For some reason, both men assume that I am from
Europe, attempting to enter the United States illegally
from Mexico. I do not tell them otherwise. Since they
have volunteered something of their family background,
I wish to reveal some aspects of my life, as honestly as I
can, and so I volunteer that I write, *soy escritora*. They
accept this, but Roberto gets right back to the basics,
saying well, that's nice, "But why don't you have papers?"

Joaquín inspects me more closely: "Can't you 'borrow' a
pass?" he asks.

Roberto answers for me: "We couldn't." Then he takes
a philosophical tone: "Those who have no papers are all
equal. *Sin papeles, todos somos iguales.*"

The two men discuss the merits of "borrowing" or
buying a pass by which one can walk across the big
bridge overhead. Joaquín relates that a friend he knew
used a "borrowed" pass but was arrested and held in
prison for six months.

Both men know many ways to cross the border. They look like they have done nothing more exciting than push pencils in an office, but each has had his adventures getting to *el norte*.

Roberto, who tells us he supports his mother and younger brothers and sisters, relates he once hid in the trunk of a car. "You have trouble breathing back there, it's pitch black and cramped and hot. But life's a struggle. What can you do?

"Sometimes they look inside the trunk when you're going through the port, but mostly they don't have the time. The one time I tried it, they looked and they caught me." But, he adds, he was not imprisoned, just sent back to Mexico.

This will be Roberto's second crossing. But his companion has crossed several times. He was born Joaquín Orestes Valdéz, in Tejolocachic, a small town near Chihuahua, the capital of the state of Chihuahua. "I first went to *los estados* when I was 14, with my married brother who had been there before," he relates.

"We crossed at Presidio in the Big Bend. It was March and very cold. We slept in the day, hiding behind bushes. And we walked at night, hoping *la migra* would not spot us. You need to know how to travel without leaving too many tracks they can follow. Although they have 'seeing' devices. And airplanes. We carried all of our food and water with us; we ate very little. We walked for six nights and eventually came to Marathon. We were there one day looking for work and they caught us."

As we talk, two women walk along the sidewalk, then retrace their steps and climb up beside us on the retaining wall. Almost immediately, they see us as "co-conspirators" and tell us they too are seeking a way to enter the States. They have come north from Durango, having heard there are jobs as domestics in El Paso. They ask me if I have worked in the homes of Anglos, and I

reply, without having to lie, that I have. We discuss the
prices that maids earn in El Paso, and to them the wages
sound fabulous. No woman makes such money where they
come from.

When I am not watching the black bridge, I study the
would-be domestics beside me. They are neatly dressed in
slacks and shirts, and carry no possessions other than
small purses. Neither of the women is rushing to divulge
case histories. No one is questioning the other. The
women are seeking a more independent life but each now
hopes to remain in this circle with its pyschological
cushions. Each hopes we can go in a certain strength
together across the bridge. Now we are five with a single
purpose. We watch the black bridge and only occasionally
speak. We think of ourselves, our problems. We do not see
the world around us. We have attached ourselves to
strangers, and they have become closer than kin.

Two hours pass. *La migra* waits on one side, the people
wait on the other. There are more people, and they have
more time. I wonder why the Southern Pacific Railway
has not barred this bridge against pedestrian traffic?
Perhaps it plans to do this. But I know that will not end
the flow of illegals. There are millions of them and they
have a million ways to cross.

It is mid-morning and steamy hot. We tire of waiting
for the Immigration car to leave. So we walk east, toward
Chamizal Park, where Mrs. Carter and Carmen Romano
de López Portillo, wives of the presidents of the United
States and Mexico, held their 1977 meeting. The park
takes its name from the Chamizal Treaty that returned
630 acres along the disputed United States border to
Mexico. At that time we lined the banks of the Rio
Grande with concrete to hold the river to the boundary.

With Roberto and Joaquín, and the two women, whose
names I've learned are Carmen Segovia and Cristina
Aguilar, we watch the sluggish river flowing through this

manmade canyon separating jobless workers from our factories and fields. Across the Rio Grande I see the large, new El Paso municipal center, the *Paseo del Norte* hotel and the bus station. The distance to El Paso is only a stone's throw or as far away as Paradise—depending on one's documents.

The two women are going up against all the difficulties that the men face plus, perhaps, a few more. I recall, studying the women, what Orendáin in San Juan, Texas, had told me about the strong-armed Texas guards: "They rape the girls that come across the border. If the girls do not cooperate with them, they will send them back. If they do, then they let them work here."

Carmen, the older of the two women, is tall, or at least she projects height. With the rearrangement of certain features, an enlargement of eyes and mouth, Carmen might have been a great beauty. She has ample bosom and hips. She wears her long, black hair tied in a bun at the nape of her neck. Her dark eyes convey the mystery of a woman's inner life and personal sadness. Yet she is quick to smile or break into laughter.

Born in 1942, the eldest of seven children, Carmen speaks of herself as already old, *vieja*. Her father once owned a plot of land he farmed with others, called an *ejido*. "But we had no machinery and no money for seeds. And my father leased the land to a big American company to grow tomatoes. He worked for that company for $1.50 a day until he fell from a tractor and injured his leg. Since then he has been unable to work. I never got married because I have always known I must help my family. I have a sister who has five children. But she has no husband, so I must help her."

Carmen's first job in Mexico was making candles. The candles were used in church ceremonies, and she laughs recalling how her friends told her she made enough candles for God to become a saint. She worked at the factory for six years, earning the equivalent of a dollar a day.

Then she went into business for herself. "I set up a little stall in a market selling tortillas and soup. But my mother said I was killing myself, so I gave that to someone else. Then I went to take care of children at an orphanage at night. But I got sick and had to leave. Then I set up a clothing business. This, again, was at the public market. I could sew, and I'd shout it out. After people saw that I could sew well, they would leave me their yard goods so I could make them dresses."

Our group continues to stroll along the embankment, the two men ahead of us not listening to the women behind. I learn that Cristina, who is petite, slender, with her black hair cropped in a casual, modern style, first came to Juárez when she was 13 to visit a maternal aunt. She stayed a summer, and returned the next year to clerk in a small store. When she was 18 she met Rigo in a dance hall. "And we got married. He was insanely jealous. I'd say, 'Rigo why do you make us suffer? I'm not flirting. I'm not going out with other men.' But he beat and tortured me, and after two years I left him. Adalberto was eight months old. I carried him in my arms and knocked on doors asking for work as a maid. It is difficult to find work in Juárez. I got a job as dishwasher. They let me keep him there in a stroller." Then, back in Durango, she left the baby with her mother and got a job at the home of a well-to-do Mexican family as a live-in maid. They paid her the equivalent of $5 a week. The family included the mother and father and seven children.

"I was told I could never go out alone. The only day I could leave the home was on Sunday, to accompany them to Mass. There was no one outside the home with whom I could visit or talk."

Cristina got up at six in the mornings and often did not get to bed until one o'clock the next morning. "I did all the cooking. And they wanted fresh tortillas morning, noon, and night." She was aware her employers thought of her as an indentured servant on whom they unloaded everything. "I made all the beds, scrubbed the floors, dusted furniture, did all the washing, all the ironing." She said she wanted to talk with the señora but "she'd always reject me. She didn't want to be on my level, she wanted me to be beneath her. She was always humiliating me. I tried to coexist with them. But I'd be put down, she'd cut me off. I felt sad, I would turn away. With the señora, you got the impression that she's a very good person, but the more you deal with her you realize that selfishness is the problem."

Cristina expresses herself carefully within her religious heritage. She does not say, as we might in English, that "the woman is selfish." Rather she implies the devil has gotten into the woman and implanted his selfishness.

Carmen, Cristina, and I catch up with the two men. We are leaning against a 50-foot retaining wall when Roberto shouts:

"Look! *Mojados!*"

Below, we see two young Mexicans at water's edge. They remove shoes, slacks, and shirts. Stripped to undershorts, holding their other clothes overhead, they begin wading through the shallow water.

We see, cruising along Paisano Drive in the far distance, a green Immigration sedan. Apparently the movement of the men triggered a sensor device. We first watch the car, then the *mojados*, who wade slowly, deliberately. Neither looks to either side. They reach the United States side of the river, and pull on pants, shirts, and shoes. Then they climb an embankment, and at the top they crawl under a fence and walk leisurely toward the freeway.

Now they see the green sedan in the distance. They

retreat slowly to the river. They've seen *la migra* but they can't be sure *la migra* has seen them. The patrol car might be on another call. But no, the green sedan heads toward them. Now they scramble back down the embankment to the river. They wait on the water's edge, reluctant to get wet again.

The Immigration sedan pulls alongside the fence at the top of the embankment. One patrolman sits in the sedan, talking on his two-way radio. The wets wait, still in United States territory. Suddenly the armed officer jumps out of his vehicle, walks on the edge of the embankment. He glares at the Mexicans. It's a game now of who will give in first.

"Get back in the water! *Métete!*" the Border Patrolman shouts, his hand resting on his gun.

Roberto says: "It will be interesting to see who tires first."

"It won't be the *mojados*," Joaquín replies. "They are by the water, they are cooler."

"The patrolman won't get his uniform wet," Carmen says. "And if he won't get in the water, he can't *force* them back."

"He can shoot them," Joaquín comments.

"Métete!" the officer shouts, louder and more threateningly. Again I think of Cortés and Pizarro who, aided by gunpowder, mastered a multitude. The armed patrolman along the border, however, is different. He is given a gun but is not supposed to shoot except in self-defense. Clearly he is frustrated by these wetbacks. How many such patrolmen, when there have been no witnesses, have climbed down an embankment to strangle a defiant wetback, or fired his Magnum revolver out of sheer frustration? No one really knows. The newspapers once reported that two Border Patrol officers gave chase to half a dozen Mexicans running across Paisano Drive. The Mexicans raced back and dived into a canal that parallels

the river, where the water is deep and fast. Officers testified one of the Mexican youths "kept going under and coming up again," but they could not save him. A crowd gathered in Mexico and began "throwing rocks the size of ostrich eggs" at the officers, crying in chorus: "You murdered him."

We hear the patrolman shouting again at the two Mexicans. He warns them "for the last time, *la última vez!*" Now the young men give up. They undress again and wade back toward Mexico. Once they're waist deep in the water, the agent, his authority upheld, returns to his sedan and speeds off. Back on the Mexican side, the two young men walk along the river to the east. Further downstream, they probably will try again.

Roberto, Joaquín, Carmen, Cristina, and I walk west. We begin to feel we have always known each other. Unanimously, we choose Joaquín as leader to find a place where we can cross.

"Up ahead, just up ahead, *arriba*," he says repeatedly. We march for two hours through debris, sand, stone, and brush "*Arriba, arriba,*" Joaquín repeats. He is like Coronado's guide to the seven cities of gold, who repeated "*arriba, arriba*" until Coronado grew impatient and slit the guide's throat.

In the distance, atop Mount Cristo Rey in the foothills of the Rockies, I see a statue of Christ. We are in an area where the country of Mexico and the states of Texas and New Mexico join, and where the Rio Grande, flowing from the Rockies in Colorado, turns east, searching its way to the sea at Matamoros and Brownsville. To the east, the border is all river. To the west, the border is all desert. We keep walking. I see two men half hidden in brush. They, too, are waiting to cross. I note their plastic bags to hold their clothes when they enter the water. Their clothes, their skin, blend with the earth. They seem almost to grow from the soil. I suggest to Joaquín: We could ask them where they plan to cross.

"No," he says, emphatically. "They're not our kind."

I stare harder at the two men. They are poorer, they have darker skin than Roberto or Joaquín. Joaquín thinks like many Mexicans: If one works in an office and has a light complexion one is somehow superior to darker-skinned people. He equates a white skin with brains and a dark skin with strength. Joaquín wants to get to a land of opportunity for himself and *his* kind, but is not concerned about others. I remember an Anglo saying: "Given half a chance, the light-skinned Mexicans discriminate more than we do."

I think of Cristina's story of her Mexican employer who would not talk with her as an equal, but kept her in a subservient, inferior role. In our earlier talks, Cristina had said the person who had meant the most to her, more than her own parents, was a teacher she had had when a small child. The teacher, she said, "talked to me as an equal, as one person to another."

I again study Carmen and Cristina, walking so confidentally toward their future. They may work in an Anglo home where the wife or the husband will mistreat them, but this is most unlikely. Most Mexican domestics with whom I had talked in our jails, arrested for entering without documents, told me they had good employers who had given them a new appreciation of their value as human beings.

Suyapa Gonzales from a small village in the state of Hidalgo was an example. A full-figured woman, she told me she had worked for an American family outside Dallas, at a place called Richardson, who paid her $75 a week. "I was baby sitting, taking care of their children. They gave me a bedroom with a private bath, all the things I needed, medicines, very good food, they treated me very well. They didn't know I had come without papers. They didn't ask."

On the other hand, I talked with several Mexican maids in Washington, D.C., who were treated like slaves by

Latino families who came here with diplomatic visas. One woman told me she worked for a Mexican family—the man an employee of the Organization of American States—who held her passport, would not allow her out of the house, and for six months did not pay her a salary. She said the man attempted to force her to have sex with him and, when she succeeded in fighting him off, would parade nude in front of her. Eventually, with the help of a Catholic nun, Sister Manuela Vencela of the Catholic Spanish Center, she made her escape.

Joaquín, Roberto, Carmen, Cristina, and I have come to an area where, across the river on the United States side, Ascarco has a smelter for copper, lead, and zinc. Studies have shown that the plant, which opened in 1887, has caused lead poisoning in an estimated ten thousand children in the two countries and is still a threat.

We walk near the river's edge. "This is a good place to cross," Joaquín says. The men turn to one side. Each of us takes off our shoes and slacks but leave on our shirts. We start out. My bare feet strike against slippery rocks on the river bottom. We keep going. Cristina gives a quick cry, then falls under. Roberto and Joaquín lift her up. Carmen and I fish frantically but unsuccessfully for her purse as it floats downstream. She may have her life's savings in that small purse. Cristina, perhaps thinking of the young son she must support, starts crying, uncontrollably.

Joaquín, to shock her from her tears, slaps her face and rebukes her sternly. "Our most dangerous moments are ahead. We must move quickly," he tells her. We go on without the purse. *La migra,* he warns, often sits waiting for wets here. And in the Southern Pacific railway yards, which we must cross, there are no witnesses to restrain anyone who might catch us. We reach shore and redress quickly.

We sprint along the railway tracks, then move in single

file across a freeway, dodging cars bearing down on us. I hear horns blaring, the screech of brakes. Has Cristina been killed? I do not look back or to either side. I do not even see the cars. I use all my strength to stay behind Joaquín.

Fear sends adrenalin rushing through my body. I no longer *think*. My body takes over. I move out of fear. I smell its odor: the hatred many white Texas police and many vigilantes feel for brown illegals they shoot with impunity. We run faster.

Carmen, exhausted, calls for help. Roberto and Joaquín grab her elbows, swing her along so her feet barely touch the ground. We come to a drainage tunnel, dry, yet large enough for a car to go through. We race into it seeing nothing but the curved concrete walls, hearing only the echo of our feet pounding on the gravel remnants of storms long past.

Coming out of the tunnel, we turn east, climb a small hill and enter a residential neighborhood. Scenes and images pass so rapidly by us they seem to be dreams. None of us has a watch, but by the sun overhead we know it is midday. All of us sense that we have dropped from one unreal existence into another. We walk along neat sidewalks, past clean-paved streets, well-manicured lawns, and expensive homes with expensive automobiles parked in front of them. We have moved from a country of poverty to a nation of wealth, and it is all around us. The transition is almost traumatic.

Joaquín has said that once we reached this neighborhood, we must go our separate ways.

"We must not be seen walking together. We must scatter now," he insists. I see the women, Carmen and Cristina, walk off together. They look as though they belong here. And the young men also look as though they will make it. They are not poor enough and brown enough to be suspect.

I walk on alone. Soon I come to a small general food and drug store. A Texan in new khakis and a cowboy-style hat gets out of his new pickup truck. He goes into the store. Exhausted, hot, unable to continue standing, I collapse under a shade tree. I see him return with packages. He turns the key to his truck, the motor purrs and music blares from a radio. He lives with ease and security, in a land of comfort and abundance, of freedom.

For a moment all that seems beyond my grasp. I am on the fringe of a dream.

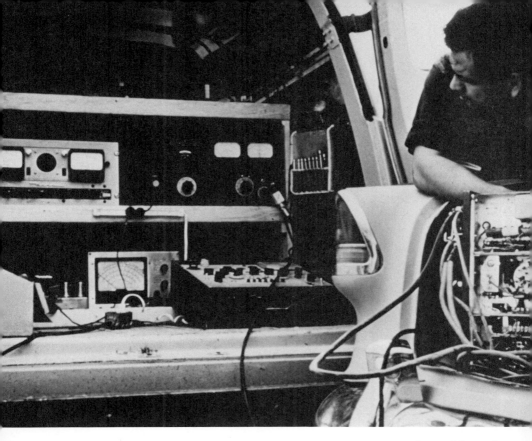

An anti-intrusion
device used by the
Border Patrol.

Another anti-intrusion
device

The green card

A border crossing card

A fraudulent card used by an illegal alien to gain entry to the United States.
(Official U.S. Immigration and Naturalization Service Photographs Washington, D.C.)

A Border Patrolman pointing out the antenna on a sensor device. *(Official U.S. Immigration and Naturalization Service Photographs Washington, D.C.)*

A farm and ranch check from the air.
(Official U.S. Immigration and Naturalization Service Photographs Washington, D.C.)

Patrolling the
border by
aircraft.

A U.S. Border Patrol helicopter on beach patrol, just north of the Mexican border near San Ysidro, California. Three men are being checked for possible illegal entry. *(Official U.S. Border Patrol photographs)*

A U.S. Border Patrol
helicopter on patrol near
San Ysidro, California.

It was attempted to smuggle thirty illegal aliens into the United States in this truck.

The thirty aliens lined up at the back of the truck. *(Official*

Illegal aliens lining up to buy worthless working cards in El Paso, Texas. They pay up to $50 for the cards.

...igration and Naturalization Service Photographs Washington, D.C.)

Illegal aliens cooking their food.

A Border Patrolman examining a hole cut in a wire fence separating the United States and Mexico.

Illegal aliens being returned to Mexico by air. Champagne was served on the flight.
(Wide World Photos)

U.S. Border Patrolman W. G. Luckey captures two illegal aliens in a sugar cane patch.
(Austin American Statesman)

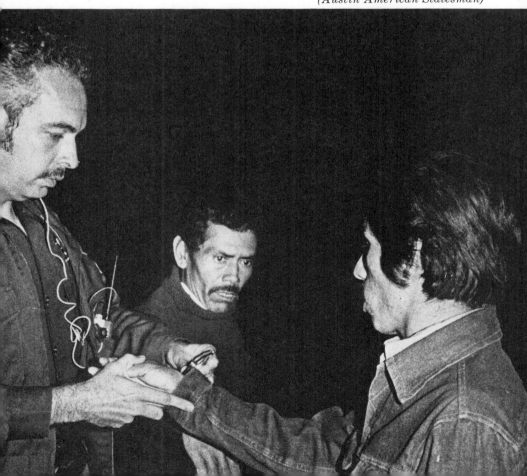

The author standing on the Black Bridge, Juaréz-El Paso.

V

Crossing
with a Pass

Once when I was a reporter in Vietnam I saw a shipload of rice in Saigon harbor, a gift from the United States. That same day I had flown over rice paddies the United States had destroyed with poisonous sprays.

We have the same ambivalence toward the Mexicans. With one hand we strengthen the Border Patrol to keep illegal immigrants out, and with the other we issue passes indiscriminately.

Once I asked Immigration officials in Washington, D.C., to give me a list of the passes most generally used for crossing. Several officers worked on the list, and they came up with ten documents. Mexicans use one card most frequently of all, however. It is called a Border Crossing Card. I asked Inspector Leo Soto: just how many of the cards have been issued?

"Over the last 25 years," he said, "more than 4.5 million."

I visualize anew the tribulations and hardships suffered by poor, unschooled *mojados* while millions of other Mexicans, shrewd enough to fill out a form, walk through our Ports of Entry with a simple Border Crossing Card.

There are several ways to secure a Border Crossing Card. One may apply to authorities, fill out the proper forms, and with good luck get the card in about six weeks. If you are not adept at writing, filling out a form, and dealing with the bureaucracy, you might borrow a card that belongs to a friend or acquaintance. Several illegals told me this is an easier way to get into the United States than swimming the river or walking across the desert. Border Patrolmen agreed.

"It's very simple to come across with a Border Crossing Card," Agent D.S. Hankin of San Diego said. "A Mexican can find a number of people who look like him. Maybe he says, 'I'd sure like to get across but I don't want to run across because they'd probably grab me.' So a cousin says: 'Go through the Port of Entry. Here, use my card.' The Mexican drives through. The inspector thinks, 'Well, it looks like him.' "

Hankin added that during the heavy rush hours inspectors do not have time to look at cards. "Everybody shows a document. As an example, we apprehended one man who said he showed a part of a cigarette package. He had it folded and in a plastic insert of his billfold. He was sitting in a back seat, and he showed that and was admitted.

"The inspectors are looking at thousands of cards in an hour and have traffic backed up for miles. From Brownsville to San Diego most of the Ports of Entry are extremely busy. The officer can barely glance at each person. He doesn't have the time to check every document."

Also, Hankin continued, "Aliens frequently come over with a Border Crossing Card and then either mail it back to their family in Mexico or have a friend take it back. Then the friend or a family member can use it. And if the alien who sent it to them is apprehended in the United States, he can claim he swam the river and likely he'll be sent immediately back to Mexico. There he can get his Border Crossing Card again, come back to the Port of Entry and be admitted for another three days. And if he mails the card back again he's off for another try."

Obviously the cards have great significance to the Mexicans.

One officer tried to explain: "Suppose," he began, "we start with a young girl. She's single, she's got a card. Then she gets married and changes her name and she applies for a new card and later she has a baby and applies to have the baby included on her card, and next year another baby.... And then, if her husband feels that the children will be crossing with him more often than with their mother he can have their names included on his card."

Apparently, the Immigration Service thought such changes were too much for them to catalogue, so they added names to old cards and willy-nilly handed out new cards.

The small laminated magical card has no expiration date and no data other than a name, photo, date of birth, and sex. As its name implies, the Border Crossing Card allows the bearer to come to the United States. But it does not specifiy when, where, or for what.

The rules are:

You must not go more than 25 miles north of the border (but you may travel as far as you wish along the border).

You must return to Mexico within three days (but no one will keep track of your crossings).

You should not use the card to cross over to work (although no one keeps track of what you do).

"I tremble every time I show the pass," admits María Montoya, the domestic with whom I lived in Juárez, Mexico. Three mornings a week she crosses to go to work and each time she shows the pass she fears it may be taken from her.

"Going shopping?" the United States border guard asks.

María nods affirmatively, hoping he doesn't recall the frequency with which she crosses. She opens her purse to show him she has the money to go shopping. "I always keep about $25 in my purse for this purpose. They treat you different if you have money," she says.

The guard waves her through. María is lucky. She's been using the same pass illegally for years.

I talked with two Mexicans who were married to United States citizens. Since marriage to a United States citizen does not automatically confer citizenship, the Mexican spouse will often use a Border Crossing Card to enter the United States. One example is Marcelino de la Osa, who lives in Juárez with his wife, a United States citizen. His wife can cross anytime, but he is undocumented and it is a criminal offense for him to do so. He used a Border Crossing Card and was caught.

"Yes," he told me, "I'm sitting here in jail. And my wife doesn't know where I am, and she doesn't have money to pay for the apartment, and she doesn't have money to give food to the babies. My sister lives in Deming, New Mexico, and she has her legal residence papers. She has seven children and they all have their papers. I am the only one who is not legal."

I also visited with a Mexican woman, Sophia Jiménez Martínez, who is married to a United States citizen. They live in Tijuana and he works in San Diego. She often used her Border Crossing Card to go to the U.S. side and meet her husband when he finished work. One day an officer looked at her card, saying:

"You must be going over to work."

"No," Sophia said, "I am going to meet my husband."
But the officer did not believe her and kept the pass.

Besides the spouses of United States citizens, I talked
with several Mexicans in jails or detention centers for
using the cards to cross. For example, Jaime Ledesma of
Nuevo León was washing dishes in a Houston restaurant
when Immigration agents raided the restaurant. They
arrested Ledesma and he was held three months in a city
jail before authorities removed him to an Immigration
Service Detention Center. He had been held there for
three weeks when I interviewed him.

How, I asked him, did the agents know he had used a
Border Crossing Card?

"I told them," Ledesma replied.

Soon after I interviewed Ledesma in prison, I talked
with a Border Patrol agent who admitted to me that he
was married to a Mexican woman he met because she
crossed over the border regularly with a Local Border
Crossing Card to work. The patrolman fell in love with
her and kept her illegally on the United States side.
Obviously, she was committing a criminal offense, and he
was aiding and abetting her.

"It wasn't, what you might say, quite kosher," he said.

But he knew he could interpret our Immigration laws
as he chose.

"Enormous powers are invested in the hands of the
Border Patrolman," Herman Baca told me. He chairs the
Committee on Chicano Rights in National City near San
Diego. He pointed out that passes have been issued by
our government to encourage Mexicans to cross the
border and go shopping, and that they had paid off
economically. "In most instances, United States border
towns get at least half of their money from Mexican
shoppers." But, he added, the government deliberately
chose to be ambiguous. This leaves Immigration free to

interpret the rules as it sees fit—keeping an open border when our economy needs cheap Mexican labor, and shutting the door when we don't.

"Our ambivalence magnifies the whole problem," he continued. "We say we want people to obey our Immigration laws, but we have a system that allows people to come in with passes and then get lost. It's never been explained to me why they issue these if there is so much concern by Congress for the unemployed here. The result is that aliens with the cards come in, not surreptitiously, but like anyone else. Our officials know full well that aliens are going to misuse these cards because of the economic conditions on the other side of the border. So there is a massive merry-go-round going on, and the people here are blind to it."

Baca also pointed to another aspect of our policy that he regards as ambivalent. "Our State Department allows about ten million foreign nationals to come here in a year with nonimmigrant visas. They come here as tourists and students for a specified time, but that is all on the honor system. Their departure is rarely recorded and perhaps a million of these aliens—most of them white people—are settled here, with no one conducting raids or searching them out."

In El Paso I talked with Chief Agent Dale E. Swancutt, an impressive, intelligent, clean-cut man, who sits straight and gives knowledgeable, straight answers. Instead of directing a Border Patrol sector, Swancutt might, in different circumstances, be managing West Point, General Motors, or the Pentagon. Swancutt, who has been with the Immigration Service since 1950, touched on this same issue. "Even if we could effectively seal off the border," he said, "we would still have about a million illegal aliens who had come here for business or pleasure or to study—those who had entered lawfully from *many* lands and did not go home. How do you control that?"

They are the ones who, unlike the landless, jobless Mexican peasants, have some money, speak some English, know how to read and write, can afford a lawyer, and can easily get lost in the big cities. No one sees them as we see the Mexican illegals, as "different" from us and a menace to our society.

It's hard to believe that our quota laws were started just over half a century ago. In my father's time, we didn't have quotas. We imposed our first immigration quota in 1921. We said a total of three hundred fifty thousand immigrants from all countries could enter annually.

Under present quota laws, we permit only twenty thousand Mexicans to come here legally each year. Preference is given to the reuniting of families or those with needed skills. But that's only a handful. Most Mexicans cannot qualify under our quota system.

After the Border Crossing Card, the most widely used document is the Resident Alien Card, the so-called "green card," which used to be green but is now a very pale blue. Four million green cards were in circulation as of 1978. With the green card you are legally entitled to work here. The patrolman who fell in love with the Mexican woman who came over with a Border Crossing Card, helped her to fill out forms to secure a Resident Alien Card, and in the meantime he married her. Even so, he said, he had to work nine months, using all his knowledge and influence, to get her a green card.

Following the Border Crossing Card and the Resident Alien Card, the third most widely used document is a Mexican passport with visa. The passport is issued by Mexican authorities and the visa is issued by the United States consular officer. No record is kept at our border station of the persons entering with the passport and visa.

You can also cross the border with a United States birth certificate or a delayed birth certificate issued on the basis of some corroborating evidence. Anyone who can read and write can send off for one of these. Or, you can have someone do it for you.

A Peruvian, imprisoned in 1977, turned perhaps eight hundred illegal aliens into United States citizens by the simple process of getting them delayed birth certificates, which they could use as a "breeder document" to obtain other identification documents, including a United States passport. The Peruvian, who represented himself as a lawyer in McAllen, got each client to sign a blank piece of typing paper on which he would write a letter to the Texas Bureau of Vital Statistics in Austin. In the letter, the client would claim he or she had been born in a south Texas town and then request a copy of the birth certificate. Since the client had been born in Mexico, state officials would find no birth record in their files. Thus, they denied the request but advised the client on procedures to qualify for a delayed birth record. They also listed 19 suggested documents that the client could use to support the birth claim. The Peruvian would then make up affidavits, forge signatures on them, and include as evidence certificates of baptism, church census records, and even notations from family Bibles.

Employees in the state vital statistics office would accept the bogus evidence and, in effect, create a new birth record in their files. Then they would mail a copy of the new birth certificate to the Mexican.

"It's amazing what can be done with birth certificates," Assistant Border Patrol Commissioner Robin Clack explained. "An individual can get a fraudulent birth certificate and then go from there. And unfortunately there is no standardized system between the states. Every state has its own system. In many cases a local municipality will file birth records. Anytime you have records you have requests for duplicates and unfortunately there's no real system for providing standardized verification."

Los Angeles County officials suspect, but cannot prove, that many of the nine hundred birth certificates issued there every day are given to illegal aliens.

Once a falsified birth certificate has been filed with the Immigration Service it can be used by other aliens. One such document, I was told, had been used 13 times, another 14 times. The birth certificate of three Mexican American brothers were used 26 times by aliens over a period of seven years.

All types of passes can be and frequently are counterfeited. The Resident Alien Card, the so-called green card, is probably the one most frequently counterfeited, since it is also a work permit.

"I've apprehended many aliens using counterfeit cards," Patrolman W.G. Luckey of McAllen told me. "There are ways for a trained man to tell. A Border Crossing card, a good one, is worth about $25. No one would want to pay more than that because it is about what it would cost to buy a real one from someone else. If you are talking about a Resident Alien Card, you can get one as low as $25 or $50. But when you start getting into good printing jobs you're talking about maybe $500 or more." As an example, an illegal woman with four children was arrested in the El Paso airport. She admitted she had sent $1,000 to a "friend" in California who had a counterfeit Resident Alien Card made for her. Those undocumented Mexican nationals who can't get papers legally, and can afford to do so, generally buy counterfeits. "Most of the illegals we get in airports have counterfeit documents," Luckey said.

A growing number of counterfeit artists are reaping untold profits selling a variety of fraudulent documents. They maintain offices in all the large cities on both sides of the border.

"Counterfeiting is a big business in Tijuana," San Diego Patrolman H.R. Williams said. "Very big. One of the roughest academy classes we've had is how to tell fraudulent documents. The more we work at learning detection, the better the counterfeiters get at it."

This, too, is part of the war on our doorstep.

But even before the plethora of counterfeit passes there was a plethora of legal passes. It was our own government that first befuddled the issue. One border guard, W.G. Hale, told me of the utter bewilderment he initially felt when he started work at Falfurrias, Texas, in 1942.

"I saw all kinds of cards and identifications," he said. "People were traveling with birth certificates, delayed baptismal certificates, passports, naturalization certificates, and citizenship certificates. I was a brand-new, young man on the job and people were handing me all of those documents to look at, and I never had seen them before. Luckily I worked with a partner, so when I was confused I was able to pass the buck."

There are so many loopholes that even after studying the rules for 40 years one top Immigration official said, "I am still confused."

Past laws as to acquired citizenship still apply today to anyone who was born during that time. If a person was born in 1940, he became a citizen under the law as it was then and is still covered by that law.

"For instance," Border Patrol agent Luckey explained, "let's consider children born overseas of an alien parent and a United States citizen parent. Prior to 5/24/34, only the father could transmit citizenship. And if the father had resided in the United States and was a citizen of the United States then the child was a citizen of the United States. As simple as that. The mother didn't count. If the mother was a citizen of the United States and the father was an alien, and the child was born outside the United States, then the child was an alien."

Luckey paused for breath, and then, delighted at showing how well he knew the law, continued:

"After 5/24/34, if both parents were citizens, and one had lived in the United States, then the child was a citizen.

"Between 5/24/34, and 1/13/41, if one of the parents was an alien, the citizen had to have lived in the United States. The child, however, had to have two years continuous physical presence between ages 14 and 28 in the United States. So if he didn't come to the United States by the time he was 26, he was thereafter an alien.

"From 1/13/41, to 12/24/52, if one parent were a citizen and one an alien, the citizen had to have ten years' residence in the United States, at least five of which were after age 16, and prior to the birth of the child."

Luckey now was warming to the subject: "Did you know," he continued, "that prior to 3/3/31, if you married an Oriental, Japanese, Chinese, or a person from India, you lost your citizenship—and never got it back? Prior to 1931, Orientals were ineligible for citizenship. Blacks could become citizens but Orientals couldn't. There's been a tremendous amount of discrimination against Orientals in the past.

"There were separate provisions for people who were born illegitimate. Now remember, prior to 5/24/34, if the mother were a citizen she could not transmit citizenship. If the kid was illegitimate, he was legitimized retroactive to date of birth as of 1/13/41. Whereas the child of the old gal who was married, he never did get to be a United States citizen.

"If a child is born in the United States, of illegal parents, the child is a United States citizen. Formerly, the child could help the parents get a Legal Residence Card. Now, however, the child can only petition for Legal Residence for his or her parents when the child attains the age of 21. It's been that way since 12/24/52."

Every Border Patrol member is given five pages of charts to determine a person's citizenship. Luckey said he had to memorize all of the classes of nonimmigrant aliens, classes of immigrant aliens, immigrating ministers, foreign employees of United States corporations, and immediate relatives of United States citizens. "I had to memorize laws pertaining to the exclusion of aliens from the United States and the law pertaining to deportation of aliens in the United States," he said.

The Immigration agent knows what no other law enforcement officer, who often arrests a "suspected" alien, knows: Our plethora of laws make it virtually impossible for an officer, other than those in Immigration or Customs, to inspect a person's documents and pass judgment on whether he is legal or illegal.

It also means that no employer would be qualified to pass judgment on whether a person applying for a job was here legally or illegally.

This inability to judge is of paramount importance because a major part of President Carter's immigration proposals would "make unlawful the hiring of undocumented aliens. . . ." Criminal penalties would be imposed against employers knowingly violating the law. The CIO-AFL's President George Meany has for many years wanted such a plan as a means of opening up more jobs to United States citizens. Employers, on the other hand, say they are not capable of judging the authenticity of the documents job seekers hand them. Some employers say that if such a law is passed they simply will not hire brown workers. Employers know armed agents will not raid their plants, offices, or fields demanding to see the documents of their white workers.

These employers are joined by Hispanic groups who also oppose this part of Carter's plan. They call the proposal "simplistic," "guaranteed to fail," and "a means to exacerbate discrimination of brown workers." The Ad Hoc Coalition on Immigration, representing ten million Hispanos, has stated: "We oppose employer sanctions.

Sanctions will unavoidably cause increased employment discrimination against brown-skinned and non-English-accented persons. Furthermore, current proposals could lead to a *de facto* national identification program for minorities only." The debate probably will grow more bitter before it is resolved.

Meanwhile, our system of issuing a plethora of passes implies a tacit agreement to permit entry to educated "illegals" and deny it to illiterates. Commenting on our immigration policy today, one INS official said, "I think we should melt down the Statue of Liberty, and instead of saying we want the poor, the huddled masses struggling to be free, we should come out and say we want the rich, the well educated, the well trained."

· VI ·

Smuggled
to the Promised
Land

In Tijuana, Mexico, across from San Diego, I live for a
while with a Mexican family and through them I meet a
Mexican named Beto Sánchez who has many contacts and
who, I hope, will introduce me to a smuggler. I swam the
border with a typical wetback and waded across with
women who wanted work as maids; now I want to learn
how a Mexican illegal is smuggled into the United States.
I have heard so many grim stories of the perils involved
in being smuggled that I fear for my life. Border areas
often are crime infested and Smugglers Canyon and the
Otay Mountains in the Tijuana-San Diego area are
among the worst for assaults, rapes, robberies, and
murders by Mexicans against Mexicans.

Earlier, in my home city of Washington, D.C., I had
met a woman called Chula from a small village near
Mérida in the Yucatán. She and two other young women,

as well as her uncle and his wife, had paid a smuggler or
coyote $500 each to arrange their trip from Mérida on the
eastern shore of Mexico to Tijuana on the Pacific coast, a
distance of some three thousand miles. Once he had them
across a broken fence and inside United States territory
near the Otay Mountains, the *coyote* beat and knifed the
uncle and the uncle's wife and assaulted and raped Chula
and her female companion. Somehow, penniless and in
their torn clothes, all of them made it to San Diego,
where they found help.

Alarmed by the high crime rate, the San Diego Police
Department created a special Task Force of Mexican
Americans to catch these bandits. I was in a patrol car
with a Border Patrolman in the Otay mountains one
night when we heard a radio report of a shooting. We
sped to the scene. The San Diego Police Department's
Mexican American policemen, who dress as Mexican
illegal aliens, were shooting it out with Mexican bandits
who had attempted to rob them. As in Vietnam, it was
hard for me to keep the good guys straight from the bad
guys because they all looked the same.

Immigration officials talk about the number of people
now being smuggled over the border and the highly
organized nature of the operation and its danger to
aliens. El Paso Chief Agent Swancutt estimates that,
except for the local commuters and those who remain
right on the border, probably half of the illegals who now
are coming over are being smuggled.

No one can know for sure, however, because no one
knows about those who are never caught. You can get
figures only on arrests. In 1977 Border Patrolmen apprehended 138,805 aliens who had been smuggled into
this country. They apprehended 12,405 persons they chose
to call smugglers. In most cases they do not catch the real
smuggler, but rather the driver of a vehicle used to
transport the aliens. The driver, called a mule, is a small-

time accomplice in a much larger network where the
ringleader remains as anonymous as a Mafia boss.

Most Immigration officials believe the smuggling of
aliens is a large-scale, highly organized operation. And
they say: "We catch only the small fry. The big ones
always get away."

Smugglers are about evenly divided between United
States and Mexican citizens. All have a common method
of operating. Many have accomplices in the United States
interviewing employers who want cheap labor. If a
person in Mexico or Colombia wants to go to Los Angeles
for a job as a shoemaker, for instance, he knows through
the smuggling grapevine whom he should contact to
arrange for transportation—and a job.

"We can't often get to the organizers of smuggling
gangs because we have so many fly-by-nighters who are
doing it to earn enough money to buy a few drugs," one
patrolman said. "They are working for somebody who is
well organized. And that person might be in Chicago—or
anywhere."

Illegal aliens pay from $50 to $1,500 to be smuggled
into the United States—the average is $500.

To get an idea of the potential profits, assume that one
of every five illegals supposedly here, or two million of
them, paid a smuggler the average amount to get here.
That would mean smugglers have picked up a billion
dollars. And this is money drained from the poorest of
the poor in Mexico. "There is as much money in alien
smuggling as in dope smuggling," Agent Bill Luckey
believes. For this reason many dope smugglers are
changing to alien smuggling. "You don't need a big cash
investment to get into alien smuggling, as is the case
with dope. Your profits will be as great, and your risk
factors much less." Judges, he adds, tend to be very
severe with dope smugglers but lenient with alien
smugglers.

"The smugglers work on both ends. An accomplice may

contact a Chicago factory who needs foundry workers. He says he can supply x number of workers at x rate of pay. The factory people know that they are hiring illegal aliens, there's no question about that," Luckey continues.

The smuggler makes big money not only on his initial take for the crossing, but in constant kickbacks. As an example, Luckey says, let us presume a smuggler solicits ten workers for Chicago. He charges $200 to $500 each. Say it's $300. That's $3,000. It includes his services for getting you across the border, and to provide a guide at a pickup point.

"Once in Chicago, the smuggler will get the aliens a shack—they'll live ten in one shack. The smuggler pays $100 per month for the shack, but he charges each alien $100 per month to live there, so he's picking up another $900 every month. Maybe he's arranged with a work foreman to provide ten workers at 7 dollars an hour to lay railroad tracks. He gives each alien only 4 dollars per hour, and keeps 3 dollars out of every 7 dollars. He's taking $120 off each alien's labor a week, raking off about $4,800 a month plus what he's making on the rent they pay."

Immigration officials also agree that those who pay a smuggler risk all their possessions and even their lives. "It's a sordid business," Swancutt says. "Many smugglers are completely amoral. Many former smugglers of narcotics deal with people like they do dope. They have no regard for human lives." Most of the poor, jobless people who use smugglers are innocent victims of a smooth-talking confidence man who convinces them to forfeit their life savings for a travel plan to the Promised Land.

The smugglers operate all through Mexico, and send their clients to various parts of the United States, including some that are not even a wide place in the road. Los Ebanos on the Rio Grande is one such place. We keep a Customs official posted there, and the official, W.G. Hale, told me smugglers had sent several groups of

Mexicans across the river there. From many sad victims he established this pattern:

"The smuggler goes deep into the interior of Mexico, locates 25 or 30 persons and tells them, 'For $1,500 American money I can get you a job in Chicago.' These people borrow and sell everything they have to get their trip to Chicago. He heads them across the border and to the cemetery near here, and then he tells them, 'Now I have to go make the arrangements—wait for me here.' He takes their money and disappears. After about 12 hours they realize they have been had. But by then they are totally depleted. Their map runs out at the cemetery. They don't know where they are. And they are afraid. Along about five o'clock in the afternoon they give up and come down here to tell me, 'We don't have any money. The man who was supposed to guide us didn't come back.' I go down there to the river and make arrangements for a free ferry ride for them. They go back to Mexico and I never see them again.

"The first couple of times it happened I thought it was a coincidence, but it's kept on happening with a new bunch each time."

I heard many stories of smugglers who promise aliens a safe journey to their destination and a job when they get there. I saw one example of this: I was with Agent Williamson at the airport in El Paso when he talked with some Mexicans, voluntarily returning to Mexico. They had given money to a smuggler who had arranged for them to work in the strawberry and asparagus fields near Spokane. They traveled twenty-five hundred miles to Spokane only to learn they had no jobs. They had gambled what to them was a small fortune, and lost.

"As long as they get their money," Williamson observed, "the smugglers couldn't care less if the man never finds a job or is half dead or dead when he gets to his destination." Williamson recalled talking with five Mexicans who had paid a smuggler $2,500 for a package plan. He guided them across the border and gave them bus tickets to Boise, Idaho—and the name and address of a farmer he said would employ them when they got there. The Mexicans began work—laying irrigation pipes—and as Williamson recalled, "They were making eight cents a pipe, which is slave labor. The smuggler undoubtedly had a contract with this farmer in Idaho calling for a rake-off of what they were earning. But the aliens don't know that. All they know is that they couldn't make enough to feed themselves while they were there, to say nothing about sending any money back to Mexico. So they quit and walked off and came back. They'd lost the money they'd paid to be smuggled up there."

One night Williamson and his partner kept watch on a certain motel. They saw a smuggler drive carload after carload of Mexicans to the motel. The next morning a driver arrived in a U-Haul truck and loaded 41 Mexicans into the small truck. Once they were on the highway, bound for Chicago, Williamson and other agents apprehended them. It was a very hot day, and when they opened the back of the truck some of the Mexicans were nearly dead from lack of air. Their trip to freedom had hardly begun. "I do not think they would have reached Chicago alive," Williamson said.

A smuggler loading a truck or van jams people in, much as the Nazis loaded Jews into railway cars to go to concentration camps. Once the smuggler has crowded the illegals in, he locks the door of the van and does not open it until he reaches his destination. This may be thousands of miles away in Chicago, or New York.

"It's like an oven back there," one Mexican who had made such a cross-country trip said. He added two of the people in his group had suffocated to death.

In one instance, a smuggler loaded a U-Haul with illegals, locked them in, drove to San Antonio, and left

the truck parked on a street for three days. An agent who
investigated the case reported some of the people kicked
their way out. Others were so ill they had to be
hospitalized.

In El Paso, agents found a tank truck filled with
illegals when some of them started beating on the sides
of the tank to attract attention. "When we opened it up,"
an agent related, "we found 22 of them were dead—
asphyxiated by the fumes."

In the Brooklyn detention center, I talked with several
Mexicans from a group of 37 who had paid a smuggler
$500 each to transport them from the state of Puebla to
Tijuana, and then through a broken fence and over the
Otay Mountains—the same area where Chula was attacked. This group got through the Otay Mountains,
however, and to a San Diego motel. There they were met
by a driver, who packed all 37 of them inside the back of a
truck and locked the door. The driver and his assistant—
stopping only for fuel—drove for three days and three
nights.

"We carried our own food, we didn't once leave the
truck to stretch our legs or go inside a cafe or a
restroom," Angelina Nuez, 20, who is three-months pregnant and traveled with her husband, told me. The aliens
used a five-gallon can for a toilet.

When they reached the outskirts of New York they
were arrested by Immigration authorities. Angelina
thought someone, she can't imagine who, tipped *la migra.*

"It's been a nightmare," Angelina said. "We came with
great expectations of meeting people, of knowing the
place, of working here, of enlarging our world—then we
have to land in jail. We lost our money, we lost everything. Some had to borrow money, now they have to
repay it. It will take several years."

After learning as much as I thought I could about
smuggling from Border Patrolmen and illegals in the
detention centers, I begin to question an acquaintance in

Tijuana, Beto Sánchez, who seems to be knowledgeable on the subject. I come to know him slowly, which is the Latino manner. And, in time, I tell him I would like to meet a smuggler.

"A smuggler of dope or people?" he asks casually.

People, I tell him.

Beto is silent. Eventually he tells me his cousin is in that business. Every Mexican, I remember, has a cousin, a *primo*, for whatever one might need. In need of assistance, the Anglo looks in the yellow pages; the Mexican goes to a near or distant *primo*. After a week, Beto arranges for me to talk with his cousin, Eduardo Burriaga. I learn that while Sánchez is a Mexican citizen, Burriaga is a citizen of the United States.

Born in El Centro, Burriaga was taken as a child back and forth across the border. His mother died and his father remarried. "I was alone in the world. I tried everything. I lived in the streets, I robbed, I stole." He ended up in a United States reform school. "I better join the Army," he told himself. "Go to Vietnam." He saw the Army as one of the few places where he could get a roof over his head, clothes, and three meals a day. It was a choice between slow death in the barrio or possible quick death on the battlefield. And, once he got to Vietnam, Burriaga discovered there were scores like him. Chicanos, he says, had a higher death rate in Vietnam in proportion to their population than all other groups of servicemen. He didn't have time to do much thinking initially, he was too busy fighting, attempting to prove his Chicano manhood. "If I could kill for this country then, I thought, the people will see me as a first-class citizen."

However, as he stayed longer in Vietnam, "I came to see I had more in common with the Vietnamese *campesinos* than with the Anglos who sent me there to kill them. First the *campesinos* had to ward off the French, then the Americans. And I recalled the Mexicans had to fight against invasions by the Spanish, the French, the

British, and the United States." He decided "my enemy
was never the Vietnamese," but this thought, he says,
blew his mind.

"War will get you, one way or another," he adds. He
ended up in a mental ward at Walter Reed Hospital near
Washington, D.C. "I didn't know who I was." On his
release, he came to Tijuana to be among his people.

Now despite his years with the United States Army,
Burriaga, in his manner as well as in his outward
appearance, remains *muy mexicano*, with dark, flashing
eyes, dark skin, straight black hair, a soft voice that
cradles words lyrically. When he sings an Augustine Lara
love song, accompanying himself on his guitar, he takes
the high falsetto. With me, and probably with other
women, he exudes softness, warmth, tenderness. Yet, I
would not want to be his enemy. I can imagine the face,
and the gun he turned to his "enemies" when he initially
saw them as such in Vietnam. While he appears for the
most part gentle, quiet, New World Indian, he also seems
to have, beneath his surface, some of the spirit of the
ancient Conquistador—ruthless, wanton, lusting for a
fight.

With Burriaga, I walk the streets of Tijuana, the
largest of Mexico's border cities, looking into narrow,
dark corridors and mysterious, cramped, shrouded shops,
all emitting strange, sometimes sensuous, often foul,
odors. The raucousness of voices and traffic noises, the
overpowering smells and congestion remind me of other
exotic, nefarious cities—of Fez and Algiers; of Istanbul
and Hong Kong, where millions live precariously for each
moment knowing they were never promised a tomorrow.

"Here, in Tijuana," Burriaga tells me, "you can find
anything: any kind of male or female prostitution, any
contraband, any kind of deal, or dope—cocaine, heroin—
any kind of gun for hire."

In order to talk to Burriaga, I often stand in the Carlos
Primero Hotel lobby, where he works as desk clerk. I

watch Burriaga as he accepts in Mexican pesos the equivalent of two dollars from a short, thin Mexican, accompanied by an overly fat woman companion. He gives the man a key and the couple walk up a flight of stairs. Burriaga is bored by this job. He is glad to talk to me about his war years and about his experiences as a guide or *coyote* smuggling aliens across the border.

Listening to him talk about his one-man operation, I recall my conversations with Border Patrolmen who told me smuggling was a highly organized operation. Yet, the Burriagas must be multiplied by the thousands. Smuggling, then, must be a business somewhat like prostitution: For every one that is part of a highly organized ring, there are a thousand or more who are individual entrepreneurs.

Burriaga tells me about the "tubes." He explains that many tubes and drainage ditches link Tijuana and San Diego because the two cities once were one, and they continue to share the same water sources.

Bandits and murderers use the tubes as hideouts, and illegal aliens use them as a passageway from Tijuana into a suburb of San Diego.

Before meeting Burriaga I had talked with Patrolman W.D. Burt, who showed me some of the tubes on the San Diego side of the border. Some are large enough for a person to stand upright, but says Burt, "I am nervous when I go in there. Some are extremely filthy." There are many smaller tubes in which Mexicans crawl. "I won't go in one less than three feet in diameter," Burt told me, adding that the Mexicans would—"and they'll crawl on their bellies for a half a mile."

Once, Burriaga showed me a tube three feet in height that he had crawled through smuggling a Mexican illegal to the United States. "You are on your hands and knees and you fear you'll never get out," he relates. "It's darker than hell. You can't see, you can't hear, you can only smell. The stench is overpowering. We both wore handkerchiefs over our noses. But even so, the smell is so bad you can hardly move."

We inspect a larger tube, big enough for a person to walk upright. Burriaga explains that Tijuana has nearly a million people and is probably the fastest growing city in the world. However, half the homes do not have sanitation. There are no public toilet facilities. So the tubes are used as public toilets. As Burriaga and I are walking inside the tube, a Mexican in his twenties, dressed in a workman's rough clothes, dashes in front of us, stops abruptly, and apologizes, *"Con permiso."* He politely waits for us to proceed, no doubt believing we also need toilet facilities. Burriaga gives a gracious "after you" flourish of his right arm, and I see the young man open his fly and proceed to urinate. Like the Japanese men and women who use the same toilet facilities at the same time without "seeing" each other, Burriaga takes no notice. He continues talking. "The smells," he says, "are bad enough here at the opening, but they get worse as you go further along."

Burriaga and I walk back to the center of Tijuana. We pass a vacant lot filled with broken glass, old tires, discarded beer cans, and other debris. "Only winos live here. Dozens of liquor stores are a block away. They don't do anything but drink," Burriaga comments. All of the major problems of Mexico are piled in a heap along our border. I recall that the wife of the president of Mexico in 1977 asked Rosalynn Carter to work with her on a plan to clean up our border cities. But very little has yet been done.

As we continue walking, I ask Burriaga: Has he ever been arrested by *la migra?* "Too many times," he says.

"Once, they got five of us just as we were coming out of some tubes. I never carry any papers. And of course the others had none. We all said it was our first time. They took us to headquarters, asked our name—we all gave aliases. They wrote up a report, then they let us go."

Burriaga also tells me he has driven a truck for other smugglers. "This is very risky, however. For some reason, if they catch a United States citizen smuggling aliens they make it harder on you than they do on a Mexican alien." Still, he says, he's been lucky the times he's been a driver. "My people, the ones I'm getting across, protect me. No one 'squeals' on me."

He recalls driving a van with 20 people. "I crossed over near the Otay Mountains, about ten miles west of the Port of Entry. Soon after I crossed I saw a patrol car. I flipped off the ignition, threw the keys out the window and hurled myself into the back of the van. The patrolmen ordered us all out and began questioning us: who was the driver, who was the guide? One man said, 'Oh, I had my head down, I couldn't see who was driving.' They all said something like that. So they never could find out. We were taken to a detention station. They kept us a week, then released us."

Later Burriaga used a different route, and delivered the 20 people across the border to the Del Rio motel. Early the next morning another driver with a different vehicle got the people into Los Angeles.

Burriaga also once worked as an arranger. "I'd get the people together here in Tijuana. I'd arrange the trip, put it together, decide how and when to cross. I might decide to move them through the Port of Entry with counterfeit papers. Sometimes we borrow legitimate cards, and match up the faces with the people we're moving across. But that takes too much time. I sometimes would move loads across Dead Man's Canyon and Spring Canyon, west of the Port of Entry. I might hire an old man and an old woman, or some young kids, and send them over the line as decoys. While the Border Patrol was busy with them, I would send in my large group and it would go across undetected."

Once Burriaga had set the scene, the "guide" enters. He picks up the assembled traveling party and guides it across the line to some prearranged rendezvous, pick-up point or "drop house," usually an inexpensive motel near the border.

"At one time or another, we've used all of those motels along Highways I-805 and I-5 that lead out from the Port of Eentry into San Diego. I would register for a room, then give the key to the guide, and the guide would put his 20 or 30 people in that one room. Maybe he would bring them in around midnight. The driver would show up about five o'clock the next morning and load them into a van. He's got a big responsibility to get them through the Border Patrol checkpoints into Los Angeles.

"We would move most of the people through on Sunday nights," Burriaga continues. "The Border Patrol stops all northbound cars near San Clemente on weekdays. But on Sunday everyone is coming out of Tijuana, getting back to L.A. The traffic is so heavy *la migra* takes down their checkpoints. We'd use scout cars with two-way radios and they tell us when to go."

Burriaga says he studied the maneuvers of Border Patrolmen the way he did the movements of the North Vietnamese. "I knew their work schedules, when they punched clocks, when they changed shifts, and when their planes and helicopters flew. And I planned accordingly."

Burriaga is like most men: He would rather talk about his life to a woman who will listen than engage in any of the so-called manly pursuits. He has not questioned my interest in his work, or asked whether I am documented or undocumented. But tens of thousands of people in Tijuana never can cross to the United States legally. And perhaps he thinks I am one of them.

One day in talking with Burriaga, I tell him I want to go with him on his next trip across the border. I have overheard his telling a friend he plans to smuggle a small group through one of the tubes. "Oh, I'd never take a *woman* through the tubes," he responds. He adds, "I don't

think you could stand it." Eventually, however, I persuade him to let me try.

The next day I accompany Burriaga to a coffee shop
with only three booths. Here I meet his other customers,
Jose, a young man in tight-fitting, modern, synthetic
trousers and silky shirt, who openly shows his displeasure
that a woman is going to accompany him, and another
man named Ramón, dressed in work clothes. His hands
have calluses and he tells me he is a farm worker. I like
Ramón, trusting—as I believe one should—to a quick, first
impression. José nervously chain smokes cigarettes and
drinks several cups of coffee. At one point he unbuttons
his shirt to the waist and fans a section of it across his
chest. He admits he's worried about *la migra* capturing
us, taking his picture, and putting him in a prison.

It's been agreed that we four will leave around midnight. Meanwhile, Burriaga wants to talk privately with
José, and the two of them take a stroll. Ramón and I
leave together, walking along crowded sidewalks, past
small shops huddling in on each other. I look into small
bars that boast big orchestras, as many men in the band
as customers in the bar. From one basement bar, a
drunken man runs up the steps, shouting in Spanish over
his shoulder, "motherfucker!" A woman's voice shouts
back at him, "You're a motherfucker, too!"

Ramón knows Tijuana well, he says. He has been here
several times for crossings. He works in the states for six
months or a year, then goes back to his village. This has
been his pattern for the past ten years. For most of his
earlier crossings, he managed on his own. But now, *"la
migra* makes it more difficult. They have many new
weapons and new techniques, so it's best to use a *coyote.*
He knows all about the working hours of *la migra.* So,
you have to hope he can outsmart them." Once Ramón hid
in the trunk of a car. Once he hiked the ten miles over the
Otay Mountains and he has crawled through the tubes.

Ramón, like Burriaga, knows the pros and cons of each tube. He, too, like Burriaga, warns me about the stench. And also, again like Burriaga, he says, "You can get robbed, murdered." But, presuming you get safely through the tube, you exit in a busy, highly populated suburb of San Diego. You can easily get lost in the crowd. Then you get a bus into San Diego, and go on to Los Angeles or Chicago from there.

On the other hand, Ramón continues, one may easily walk across a Tijuana freeway, jump a fence and forthwith you are standing in *el norte*, without suffering the wretchedness of crawling through a drainage ditch.

"But you still have to walk through Smugglers Canyon, and it's like a mine field, filled with sensors and other electronic traps *la migra* brought from Vietnam," Ramón tells me. Also, "It's a hiding place for bandits, robbers, murderers. You can be assaulted, robbed—killed." He makes this stretch of United States property, so near one of the nation's most beautiful cities—San Diego—sound like a grim, sinister, no man's land filled with more ghastly, forbidding obstacles and frightful characters than Dante's purgatory.

One hesitates to believe such a war zone exists within the United States. Even the Mayor of Tijuana found the grim stories he had heard about the robberies and murders of Mexican citizens immediately across the boundary line hard to believe. To investigate at first hand, he dressed as a poor Mexican alien, crossed the line that separates our countries, and no sooner had he arrived in Smugglers Canyon than he was attacked, beaten, and robbed.

Ramón and I return to the San Carlos Hotel, killing time until midnight. Burriaga and José join us and we stand on the walk outside the hotel. A vagrant sleeps at our feet. Police sirens wail and in an adjoining bar armed officers arrest a man they said was wanted for murder.

Evil and death swirl around us, and, amidst it all, innocent people step through the deprivation, glad to have lived another day.

Burriaga tells José that I have said he is scared. "I'm not scared," he protests. Then I tell Burriaga he shouldn't have told José that. "It's important we all know how each feels," Burriaga replies.

I attempt to placate José: I didn't say he was scared, just nervous. And I add I'm nervous too. To prove my point I reach out and touch him. It is a hot night, and my hands are icy cold.

"We shouldn't be talking so loud like this," José says. "I fear the Mexican police. If they arrest us, it will be worse than *la migra*. I once worked as a policeman. I know how tough they can be. They'll throw you in jail and you can stay there forever."

The thought sends a chill over me. I am with strangers in a foreign country with no identification of any kind. I could not prove my name if my life depended on it. I would, indeed, be very suspect, dressed in old denim pants, an old shirt, with no relatives or known address in Mexico, and only 50 cents in my coin purse. My pleas might sound breezy and implausible. Mexican police could easily throw me in jail and ask questions later. Ten years later.

Burriaga calls us into the hotel lobby. It's nearly time to leave. He tutors us, as a teacher before an exam. "If we're caught, what do you tell *la migra?*"

"I am Guillermo Zapata," José answers.

Burriaga turns to me. I don't know. Shall I be Dolores or Graciela—or Chela?

"Be Chela," Burriaga says. "It's short and you can remember it."

Eventually it's midnight and the four of us leave the hotel and walk toward the border. Burriaga tells us the route we'll take, and raises his right arm to point in the direction of the tube. "Don't point!" José pleads. "You look like you're signaling *la migra!*"

But Burriaga, who can't talk without his hands, keeps pointing, and says we must cross the highway two by two. We discuss who will go first. José, who has been overly anxious for hours, wants to go first. Ramón says he will accompany him. They are to go to the entrance of the tunnel, and wait for us. Then we will all crawl through together. Traffic swirls around us as Burriaga and I watch José and Ramón walk in measured, determined steps across a busy thoroughfare called Scenic Drive that parallels the border. When they have crossed, Burriaga and I follow. We try to look like any other pedestrians, but apparently we don't.

A car filled with Mexicans speeds by, a youth leans out, shouting, "Hey, *mojados!*" We get across the highway and quicken our pace, walking in a ditch alongside Scenic Drive and near a fence that separates the two countries.

Still, we are in Mexico. Suddenly Burriaga and I see a Mexican police car cruising in our direction. We drop face down in the ditch. We cannot shout a warning to José and Ramón, who, facing us, do not see the police. Two uniformed men jump from the car and seize them. Burriaga and I remain face down in the dirt. We barely breathe.

Gingerly I raise my head. The Mexican police are questioning Ramón and José, who drops his head on his chest. Ironically what he feared most, arrest by the Mexican police, has occurred. Apparently the police have not seen us.

"We'll never make it to the tube," Burriaga whispers. "They'll be watching that."

I lift my head again slightly as the police lead José and Ramón to their sedan. "We better get out of here," Burriaga says.

Like furtive animals we crawl from the ditch and under

a ten-foot cyclone fence. In a second, without risking the tubes, we are on United States territory, out of Mexico, safe from apprehension by the Mexican police. But now we must walk through the dread Smugglers Canyon.

We are moving rapidly toward a crime-infested section in the canyon called the River Bottom when headlights suddenly flash on us.

Burriaga warns, *"La migra!* They've seen us." We start running. We are in a zone where Customs officials check trucks and their cargo. Vehicles with approved cargo sit there overnight.

A large truck looms on one side of us. I tell Burriaga: Let's hide in here!

"It's locked for sure," he says, but I try a door, and miraculously it opens. We throw ourselves into the cab. Burriaga closes the door. Three police cars pull up.

I am out of view, lying on my right side. Burriaga, too, is on his right side, his head on my left thigh.

My heart learns a faster beat. I listen to men we fear: armed men, with guns, knives, walkie-talkies, scopes, helicopters, sensors—the same arsenal of weapons that I had seen in Vietnam. Now, however, I am one of the enemies.

Burriaga is my only defense against the brutal tactics I fear they will use if they find us.

"We know you're under there," one agent calls out in Spanish. "You bastards, we've seen you, come on out!" They have seen us only from a distance and so they must have mistaken me for a man. Their huge flashlights penetrate under each of the trucks, but never inside the cabs. Obviously they think the drivers have locked the cabs of their trucks in one of the worst crime areas in the world.

"Don't move," Burriaga whispers. I know he means don't say a word, don't take a deep breath. I melt into the seat.

"How many of the bastards did you see?" one agent calls to another. I hear another asking headquarters for helicopter surveillance.

"I saw four but the Tijuana police got two. Probably robbed them and threw them across the line," a voice responds.

"Damn! They've got to be under one of these trucks," an angry and frustrated voice says. I hear feet tramping, walkie-talkies squawking, car doors slamming.

Each moment I expect the truck door to be pulled open, a long, strong arm to grab me and hurl me to the ground. I know the armed men will not see me as a citizen with inalienable human rights, but as a brown-skinned fugitive whose future lies in their hands.

Eventually, we hear two police cars leave. I raise my head just enough to look out the right window. I see a green Immigration van. Men outside it search through the grass, using walkie-talkies and flashlights. The van has radioed to a helicopter, and now it's overhead. It moves, hovers over the trucks, illuminates them with powerful lights. The two police cars we heard leave now come racing back to the scene.

"They're *all* coming back!" Burriaga whispers.

Hide ... and seek. Burriaga and I are so ridiculously outnumbered! We are like ants being chased by a herd of elephants.

"The sonsabitches must have gone into the tube," one officer shouts.

"We'll catch them when they come out," a voice answers. He radios other agents to watch for two wets coming out of the drainage ditch in San Ysidro.

At last the cars leave. Finally, Burriaga sits up. And I move from my pinned-down position.

For the first time in an hour I realize that I have another identity, that I am hot a fugitive illegal, hiding.

"Let's make our move!" Burriaga says. We slip down

from the truck cab and walk to a busy highway, Interstate 5, and across a bridge called Avenida Camiones. Now we are on a typical United States thoroughfare. So much, so close. Too close to that other world with its jobless, hungry mass, its squalid, unsymmetrical, cardboard houses. Here one sees the orderliness, the paved streets, the sidewalks, the neatly rowed homes and offices. The bright lights. The big cars. The abundance is both an invitation and an affront.

As Burriaga and I walk, we see the symbols of the American Way: McDonald's, Jack-in-the-Box, Trave-Lodge, Colonel Sanders Fried Chicken, Greyhound, Shell. Open-air cafes are brisk with business. People are sitting outside, drinking coffee or cold drinks, eating hamburgers, licking ice cream cones. They seem indifferent—they must be—to the world of Have Nots just across that fence.

Burriaga and I have not eaten all evening. Does he want a coffee?

"No," he says, "I'm worried about José and Ramón." I don't have to ask; I know he intends to go back to Tijuana to learn if they are in jail.

We say goodnight. I walk a few blocks to a bus station and go to San Diego, where I am staying with some Catholic sisters. It's 3:30 in the morning when I take a key from under a mat, unlock the door, and slip into the nuns' home at the Communities of the Holy Spirit. Quietly, I steal up steps to my room. Exhausted, I try to sleep. But I toss helplessly.

I hear brakes outside. It's the police, looking for me! Or *la migra* coming to knock on the door. Is that the drone of a helicopter overhead? Every sound is ominous. Fear grows inside me.

VII

The Border Patrol

"I'm in the Border Patrol for the danger. I'm just a kid at heart." This is W.G. Luckey, Jr., speaking as we cruise along the Rio Grande searching for wets. A six foot three, husky, 33-year-old, born in Temple, Texas, now living in McAllen, Luckey relishes wringing the heads of rattlesnakes, hunting big game, and racing motorcycles and other souped-up vehicles. Power enthralls, the power of a man and his toys.

"This maxi-van will do well over 100 miles an hour, it has a 454-cubic-inch engine. It's got good acceleration. It'll throw your eyeballs back into your head. I've had it going so fast in a high-speed chase the speedometer climbed all the way around to five miles an hour. I figure I was doing 115. It'll keep up with most pickup trucks and most cars.

"There was a high-speed chase at Eagle Pass," Luckey

recalls. "This alien was in a sedan, one prior to 1970, without the pollution equipment. They'll do 135. And he wouldn't give up, tried to run the officer off the road. They went smashing into each other at 120 miles an hour, up and down the road and off into the bar ditch and back onto the road. Finally," he adds, eyes aglow with vicarious thrill, "the alien's car caught on fire and the officer çaptured him."

Luckey plainly wants more action in his life. "I would like to be an international mercenary, go where there is danger. I would like to go to Rhodesia. And I would like to go to Israel." Somewhere, he adds, where there is a lot more action, danger, fighting—where there is a real war.

Luckey, however, is a family man, married to "a good looking woman," Yvonne, whom he met when she was sitting in an Austin restaurant in a halter and a pair of white shorts. "And I thought she had the best pair of legs I had ever seen." Courtship and marriage followed, and they have two children, Sheri, ten, and Weylan, seven.

Luckey is strikingly handsome, with a hearty laugh and the confident personality of one who knows his worth. His prematurely gray hair adds distinction to a youthful face. Like other patrolmen, he works various shifts, but he prefers night river duty because there's more action, more excitement, more danger. "At night," he adds, his chest expanding, "I wear my bullet-proof vest."

My tape recorder sits on the seat, between us, atop a current issue of the magazine, *Guns*. "Most rattlesnakes I've seen are around the Port Isabel Detention Camp," Luckey continues. "The camp there has to have a rattlesnake-proof fence. Around here we don't get so many rattlers because the black snakes, or indigos—they can be eight feet long—swallow the rattlers whole." For relaxation his pals enjoy wringing the heads of snakes. "You take 'em by the tail and keep wringing till their heads flop off." They also like to hunt. "It's a lot of fun, you go out and burn up a lot of ammunition. This last year three other officers and I went to Kerrville and hunted for a day and a half and every one of us got a buck. Came home drinking beer and having a real good time. I wish I could hunt on the King ranch, but they have their own security force and don't let outsiders in there. Rumors are that any poacher caught there disappears."

Luckey likes variety. For instance, "Sometimes we organize a 'pussy posse' and go out at night with some of the sheriff's men and city police and round up 150 illegal Mexican women in the small bars. Of course, there's not much we can do with them. There are no detention centers for women. We put them in the county jail, write them up, and then release them." Still, it's a bit of a diversion for the men.

How many of the illegals in this Texas area are women? I ask him.

"About 1 in 20. We caught four this morning."

We pass a swampy field and the scene evokes his memories of a chase for illegals: "It was raining and we came down here with our lights off, and we were looking with our binoculars. I told my partner, 'I can see somebody down there by the gate.' And he said, 'Yeah, me too. They musta heard us.' We whipped on our lights and drove right into the gates and five people came walking up to the car. Soon as I stepped out and they saw my uniform they scattered like a covey of quail. I took off after one down this road for 50 yards—he ran out of both shoes and from under his hat. I chased him into the brush, where he fell down and I caught him!" He ends with a triumphant note. Then adds, "The others scattered and escaped."

Luckey explains the large size of many patrolmen helps create a "shock effect" on small Mexicans and has saved them from getting shot several times. "We got many people with guns in their pockets. They didn't have an opportunity to use them because they were so shocked that suddenly, right out of the middle of the night, we were towering over them. I had a fellow pass out on me, near La Grulla. He was talking to a friend of his. We jumped out of the brush, flashed our lights, and shouted at them, all at the same time. The guy screamed bloody-murder, his legs got wobbly, and he passed out. When he came to, he was relieved to find it was two officers and not two big monsters that had gotten him."

Formerly the Border Patrol specified it wanted big men. "When I came in you had to be five feet seven, with weight proportional to height. Now, because of Civil Rights rulings, and hiring of women, they have had to lower the standards. There are no height and weight standards at all. The only requirements are that you be in good physical condition—good eyesight, good ears. You have to be 35 or under when you enter duty."

Luckey went to the Border Patrol Academy for four months to study Spanish, immigration and nationality law, arrest procedures and forms, as well as training in firearms and physical conditioning. "You have to run four-and-a-half miles in less than an hour. Many when they finish can run it in 27 minutes, and that's a good clip." Luckey says he has set up a home course of a mile and three quarters, "and I go out every day and run it in 15 minutes."

We drive through an area called the Nueces strip. Luckey knows enough about our nineteenth century land grab of the Southwest to tell me "this land was involved in disputes between the United States and Mexico."

Has he ever traveled in Mexico? I ask.

"No, they won't let me travel down there with my gun. And I won't go if I can't take my gun. I don't trust these people."

We are traveling west from McAllen toward the small

community called La Grulla. "Most of the people here have something to do with dope traffic, or they're complaisant about it," Luckey says. "See that small house, with the shed in back? The man who owns that house allowed smugglers to hide marijuana in his shed back there. We sent the man to jail."

A man comes out of the shed.

"That's him now," Luckey comments. "Must have gotten out of jail."

The village is so typically Mexican, I tell Luckey, I feel I am in Mexico.

"You almost are," he says. "It's just across the river."

Circling back to McAllen we pass a vegetable packing plant.

"They don't like Immigration," Luckey comments.

Because they hire illegals?

"Right. We caught 26 aliens clipping onions right there. Captured them to a man."

Now we are driving by the river along a levee. Suddenly Luckey jams his brakes to a stop. *"There's a wet right there!"* he shouts, and leaps from the van. I climb down from the cab and walk to the river embankment. I see an inflated inner tube, and a plastic bag used for carrying possessions. The plastic bag has been neatly folded. I hear Luckey thrashing through the maze of tangled brush, tall grass, and trees.

He searches and I wait by the inner tube. I recall my crossing near this same area, with César Guerrero Paz. And I recall seeing our big, uniformed, booted soldiers thrashing in the brush in another war halfway around the world. We poured billions of dollars and lives into our "search and destroy" missions but little brown-skinned men eluded us like ol' brer rabbit in the briar patch. We can never teach brilliant Anglo men in a police academy how to win against a people who fight on their own turf— and the ancestors of the *mojados* were the first men to crawl and hide and walk in the sage, mesquite, oleander, scrub, and cactus country. They were the first to see the Rio Grande. Luckey may drag out this wetback, but the next three, four, or five—we can only guess the number—will elude him.

Luckey returns, dragging a man half his size as one would a half-drowned cat, by the scruff of the neck. "I caught the little devil," Luckey announces. The illegal looks dazed, his dream trampled. His hair is disheveled. His head hangs down.

I look at the man's ragged pants and shirt. He shrinks before my gaze, his pride going out of him. He appears a midget beside his captor.

Luckey unlocks the back of the van and thrusts his prisoner into the caged compartment. I know the *mojado* could have been Guerrero or me. Across the Rio Grande in Mexico I can hear the voices of youngsters playing in a soccer field. To the north I can see gray-gauze cotton fields in bloom. For a moment it is silent.

Then we continue driving along the levee. By radio we hear a dispatcher saying a Border Patrol plane has spotted an alien. "He's wearing blue levis and a red shirt." I see a man with a red shirt walking, then running, along the levee. He dips out of sight into the heavy brush. Meanwhile, a patrolman radios he's on the scene.

The surveillance plane drones overhead. The pilot circles, telling the patrolmen—including Luckey—to look for a man in a *flowered* shirt in an area bounded by a small gulley and a telephone pole. I imagine myself hiding in the grass, waiting for a boot to stomp on me, a monster-sized man to grab me by the nape of my neck.

Luckey and other patrolmen trample up and down the gulley, checking every bush. Then one shouts, "I've got 'em!" And six expensively-trained agents come forth dragging a pint-sized, brown-skinned man, wearing the remnants of a flowered shirt. One patrolman has ripped the shirt half off, and beneath it we see a red shirt. The captured Mexican explains he came along the levee in his red shirt, then put his flowered shirt over it, hoping this might confuse the pilot who spotted him from the air.

An agent takes him, as well as the alien Luckey captured, into headquarters. Luckey and I continue cruising.

"You wouldn't have much of an immigration problem," Luckey says, "*if* there was no reason for them to come here. Jobs are the crux of the problem. Once we fix it so there are no jobs here for them, then we will eliminate our fraud and our immigration problems. But we've got to take away the lure, the bait, that's bringing people over here."

Suddenly Luckey's gaze is riveted on another "suspect"—a lone woman walking down a farm road ahead of us. "I better check her," Luckey says. She has turned off the road, into a pasture. "I may have to run her down." He blows the horn. She turns, waits for him. He gets out of the car, approaches her. She smiles a greeting. He shows his badge and asks to see her papers. I wonder what the average United States citizen would show to prove he or she is a citizen. Here in the Valley, as in Soviet Russia or Red China, tens of thousands of brown-skinned people carry a card to prove who they are or go to jail. The woman produces a "green card," that states she is a legal United States resident.

Luckey returns to the van. And we continue our drive. We pass Mission, La Joya, Sullivan City. At Los Ebanos we turn onto another country road, toward the Rio Grande and the international ferry. Walking toward town, from the river, we see a young man on the road, alone. Luckey drives up beside him, talks to him through the window of the van.

"Good morning, how are you?" he asks, and then comes the rest of the greetings. All that is spoken and all that is not spoken by the authority of the emblem on the federal vehicle, by the authority of Luckey's badge, by the authority of Luckey's gun. It is Power that asks: *Who are you? I assume you guilty until proven otherwise.* The brown-skinned traveler pulls out his carefully guarded documents. He, too, is a legal resident of the United States.

If he stopped me on a street, I tell Luckey, I could not prove I was a United States citizen. Yet, if the young man were unable to prove he was here legally, Luckey would have taken him into custody. "Yes," he agrees. "We are the only law enforcement agency that can pick up someone and never take him before a judge. We have to believe in our own judgment."

What, I ask, are his guidelines for interrogating a woman or a man? By what criteria does Luckey see a person and act on the assumption he or she is an illegal?

"Our primary clientele is the Mexican alien. At the airports, for instance, they are usually nervous, they don't look to the right or the left, and usually they will not show up at the counter until just before the flight leaves. This gives them less chance of being picked out. They won't speak any English when they are checking in. They won't go and sit in the security area. They'd rather wait until the flight is on its last call, then they rush through. They generally do not have any baggage."

Countless thousands of white travelers also race through airport corridors, I remind Luckey. And more often than not, I do not carry baggage; it's been checked.

I recall that Joe Garza, office manager of the Port Isabel Detention Camp, said a Border Patrolman stopped and interrogated his daughter, Edna Garza de Muñoz, as she was boarding a plane from Harlingen to San Antonio. "She was furious. She wrote to Congressman Kika de la Garza in Washington to complain," Garza said. "Then a week later, her husband, Joe Muñoz, was stopped on a trip from Harlingen to San Antonio. He was in his shirt sleeves, without luggage. They mistook him for an alien."

"Nine United States citizens or persons who are here legally are interrogated for every illegal we catch," Luckey admits. Still, he attempts to adhere to guidelines he's been taught in the academy. "One thing I always look for: a Mexican individual who is wearing all brand new clothes, new shoes, new belt, new trousers. The ones from the interior wear some outlandish shirts—they'll buy them over here. They just look Mexican.

"Mexican clothes don't look like United States clothes, their yellows, their greens, their reds are all a different hue, they are rather dull compared with ours."

When he says *"They just look Mexican"* does he mean the passenger or his clothes?

"The clothes," he replies.

But hasn't he said many illegals buy new stateside clothes?

"If the clothes are bought in Mexico, they look Mexican. However, if the clothes are all new, you assume he's crossed over and bought new pants, new shirts—everything new."

Many legals also have new clothes, I suggest.

"It's rather hard to articulate the ways that you pick them out," Luckey admits. "You develop a sixth sense."

Some judges now hold that the Immigration officer must be able to show "probable cause" or "articulable facts" for accosting a person and demanding he prove his citizenship. In Illinois, for instance, the Immigration Service is under an injunction from a federal district court saying that an agent cannot talk to any person without "probable cause." This means, Luckey explains, "that unless I *know* in my own mind that a guy is an alien, I can't accost him." Should the Illinois judge's ruling be applied in Texas, the Border Patrol could not have its agents at the airports, because, as Luckey says, they could not prove probable cause for interrogating certain passengers. This would also be true for their accosting brown people all along the border. Such an injunction—to show probable cause for arresting persons—would interfere terrifically, he said, with their work.

"But here in Texas," Luckey continues, "if I see someone who looks like an illegal alien to me, if I *suspect* he is an illegal alien, I am empowered under Section 287 of the Immigration and Naturalization Act to interrogate him. Just like I stopped the man who was walking down the road from Los Ebanos. I'm empowered to do that. If I had been in Illinois, I couldn't have stopped that man. I couldn't tell if he was an alien. He looked as if he *might* be one. But it was just a suspicion on my part."

Increasingly, brown-skinned Mexican Americans resent being seen as "suspect" people. In Salem, Oregon, the Mexican community has filed a civil suit against the Immigration Service. The suit demanded an injunction that would stop Border Patrolmen from detaining them simply because of their skin color or language. In Chicago several Mexican American organizations, including CASA/General Brotherhood of Workers and Latin Women in Action, have urged the community to refuse to submit to identity checks by Immigration agents or the local police.

Legal as well as illegal workers are joining in opposing any new program they fear will empower federal agents to harass brown-skinned persons. A conference of Mexican workers and labor leaders in San Antonio supported a campaign in which citizens of both Mexico and the United States will refuse to present documents to Immigration agents. The conference followed an example set by Mexican women working at a San Antonio garment factory. During an Immigration raid, the women refused to show their documents. One of the women who resisted said, "I was born in the United States, but if they ask me for papers I will not show them anything. They cannot treat us like criminals."

Roman Catholic Bishop Raymundo Peña of San Antonio told me that Border Patrolmen along the Rio Grande interrogate and harass not only undocumented workers, but anyone with brown skin. When he was a Laredo priest, he frequently traveled to Robstown in Texas to visit his parents. "I was often stopped by the Border Patrol and they would demand proof of my citizenship. They were very, very rude. And they do this regularly," he said. "They stop the cars on the roads and if you look like you might be Mexican, they'll interrogate you."

Soon after I talked with the bishop, I boarded a bus to travel along the Rio Grande. Throughout the Southwest, the Immigration and Naturalization Service maintains checkpoints, where all vehicles are searched. Outside Laredo, the bus was stopped at one of the Border Patrol checkpoints. An armed patrolman came aboard. "Got any illegals?" he asked the driver. I had swum across the Rio Grande without papers, and technically was "wet."

"I can't swear to it," the driver responded.

The patrolman scanned the passengers, looking for suspects. How does he judge when to interrogate a person, force that person to prove his citizenship? If the person is light skinned, well fed, and well dressed, he automatically passes inspection.

"They look okay," the patrolman said to the driver, and disembarked. We continued west.

From McAllen, it is almost a thousand miles up river to El Paso. The Juárez-El Paso area has the second largest number of illegal crossings, after Tijuana-San Diego. In El Paso I visit with Chief Patrol Agent Swancutt who says the big influx of Mexican aliens began when our bracero program was abolished. "They had got used to a way of life. They weren't content to go back to Mexico and remain there. They were schooled in our ways. They knew how to cross the line, and so they started coming back."

In the beginning, most illegals went into farm work but that no longer is the case. Beginning in the 1960s perhaps as much as 99 percent of the aliens—except for what Swancutt calls local commuters—go to the large cities, because, he says, not only is the pay greater but their chances of being located are much less. "If they can get to Chicago and stay out of trouble they can practically remain as long as they wish, undetected."

Swancutt says the number of illegals arrested in his sector—one hundred fifty thousand in 1977—increases every year. And, he adds, "the incidence of armed encounters and physical resistance to arrest is escalating in like proportions." Patrolmen along the line with Mexico "are exposed to constant rock throwing—and now even sniping." In turn, he says, the agents get tougher, using "whatever force necessary to effect the arrests." He predicts increased violence.

Moreover, he does not see the Carter Administration coming close to any solutions. Big pronouncements on giving the Border Patrol additional resources and more manpower were designed to "appease the public" he feels, adding: "But that is not the answer."

He stresses what is clear to anyone who knows our border with Mexico: "You cannot control the flow of illegal aliens into the United States by any law enforcement method. It's impossible because of sheer numbers. If you ask me how many men I need in this sector to control the problem, I couldn't tell you. Armed agents would have to be on the border hand to hand. And that is tantamount to having a police state, and there isn't anybody who wants that. I don't. I don't see more men on the border as any answer.

"Now, I'm no different from any other law enforcement chief. I would like to have more technology, all sorts of equipment. But that is not any long-term solution to the problem. And anyone who thinks it is, just really doesn't know."

He points out that some millions of aliens enter the United States lawfully every year in the various nonimmigrant categories, and about ten percent of these aliens of all nationalities do not go home. So he stresses, "if you look at the illegal alien problem in its total spectrum you'll find you are dealing with many nationalities. We talk about Mexican nationals because of our proximity to Mexico here. We apprehended about a million illegal aliens in 1977. Almost 90 percent were Mexicans. But that does not paint a true picture. It simply means that we are located right here on the boundary and our objectives are to apprehend as many as we can before they get to the interior of the United States and find employment. So naturally we apprehend large numbers of Mexicans and other Hispanics."

Mexicans also are easier to apprehend than white-skinned aliens. "They have historically gravitated toward certain enclaves, or *barrios,* and to certain types of employment so they're easier to locate. The Canadians or European aliens don't do that, and they are more difficult to locate. Because of this," Swancutt adds, "I really dislike to single out the Mexican alien." But then, as he admits, the Border Patrol is almost totally geared toward arresting Mexicans.

The next evening Swancutt arranges for me to go on night patrol with one of his agents, Harold Williamson. Recalling my experiences bumping over levees and country roads with Patrolman Luckey, I dress in khaki pants and a sweatshirt—and arrive at Border Patrol headquarters to meet a man six feet, five inches tall, and so nicely dressed in a new, navy-blue civilian suit he could be taking me out to a cocktail party. I comment on his attire and he explains it's not his night for the bush.

We walk outside to his sedan. Then drive to the Paisano Drive along the Rio Grande. It was across this busy freeway, several miles to the west, that I had crossed with two illegal men and two illegal women who wanted to work as maids.

As Williamson, who is called "Big Willy," and I cruise along, we see on the opposite side of the highway, by the river, a United States Customs car spinning its wheels in the sand. Customs officials, like Border Patrol agents, also search for illegals in a duplication of effort that our government is now investigating. "Let's see if they need our help," Williamson says, pulling over on our side of the highway. Before he can get out, however, we hear a Customs officer call across the river to some young Mexicans swimming on the Mexican side to help them push the car out of the sand. The young Mexicans quickly swim across and extricate the car. Then they swim back.

Williamson and I continue on our way. The Mexican youths were not "legal," I comment. Yet the Customs officers had asked them to swim over. They had, in fact, encouraged them to break a law. Williamson says that probably the Customs men didn't think of the law; like you or me, they thought of their problem at hand.

In countless instances like this, we call to the Mexicans, never thinking we are establishing habits that will be hard to break. Another example: I have seen soccer fields on the United States side of the border. "They are not bothering anyone," Border Patrolmen say of a youths who cross the line to play ball. Should a youngster decide to leave his play and take a job, however, he could be sent to Leavenworth. Actually, he breaks our law every day he crosses to play ball.

Every day, Williamson tells me, agents in his sector apprehend 300 to 400 illegals.

We pass railway yards. Nodding toward the freight cars, Williamson recalls, "Once we got 20 in one bunch. Walked them out." As he says this, he sees movement under one of the trains. Abruptly, he slams his brakes, cuts the ignition, jumps from the sedan, and dashes into the darkness.

I get out and, standing near the car, watch him corral three small boys who look about ten years old, none of them standing as high as Williamson's waist. Each carries a shoe-shine kit. Williamson puts them in the back of the car and we drive to headquarters, where he interrogates them in Spanish.

What are their names? Leo Arreola, 9, Juan Gonzales, 10, and Francisco Ramírez, 12. Where in Juárez do they live? Where are their parents? The children seem not to know how to respond. But gradually it emerges that they are orphans and that they earn their way in life by giving shoe shines. To increase their fortunes they were setting out to catch a freight car. I look at their possessions. Each set out for the trip with a few bottles of black and brown shoe polish and the equivalent of 25 cents.

"Where were you going?" Williamson asks.

"Wherever the train was going," Francisco, the eldest, replies. Neither Leo, Juan, or Francisco go to school. They are street urchins, destitute, illiterate. Yet when I talk with Francisco, I see a face ennobled by a dream. A certain light in his eyes indicates he will try again and somehow will make it the next time or the next. He may be one of the survivors in a system that crushes the next thousand like him.

Williamson leaves the boys at the Border Patrol office where they will be walked back to Mexico, and we return to his car. As he drives along, looking for more aliens, Williamson grows reflective. He ponders whether he might not have seen Leo, Juan, or Francisco when they were infants. Some of the teen-age aliens he apprehends today were children he saw back in 1963 when he began work. "They were two or three years old and were coming over with their older brother or sister, and they'd beg here on the streets of El Paso. You'd ask them where their parents were, and they'd say in Mexico, and you'd ask them why didn't they stay home, and they'd tell you: Their father or their mother sent them over here to beg, and told them not to come home until they had enough money to make it worthwhile. If some older kid didn't rob them, their parents would take their money when they got home."

Williamson, who has a Mexican American wife—and several agents do—thinks of his own children. "And sometimes," he adds, "it's actually kind of hard to send them back, knowing that if they go home without any money they are going to get beaten or at least scolded by their parents, and turned around and sent back here. So there's more involved to the problem of the illegals than just going out and catching ol' Joe Wet out there."

At the El Paso airport, I watch Williamson standing in the last corridor leading to a plane. In his blue suit, he looks like an airline employee checking passengers. If you are white skinned, with blue or green or hazel eyes, he lets you pass, you need not worry about being asked to prove you are a United States citizen.

He stops three dark-skinned men, pulls out his badge to identify himself, and demands that each prove his right to be here.

"We are from Kuwait," one of the men replies in good English. Each shows documents stating they are assigned temporarily at Fort Bliss near El Paso. Later, we walk to the airport lobby, and Williamson sees two more dark-skinned men. Again he accosts them, flashes his badge, and asks them to prove their right to be here. Again one of the brown-skinned men is from Kuwait, stationed at Fort Bliss. His companion, a United States citizen with brown skin, complains angrily: "What right do you have to interrogate us? You stopped us only because our skin does not happen to be white." "No, no," Williamson protests.

Later, I recall that Williamson has told me his wife is of Mexican heritage. I ask: Was she ever stopped at an airport and asked to prove she was legal?

"Not that I know of," he replies. But surely, I insist, he would know. He does not give me a yes or no answer, but volunteers: "I think of her as a United States citizen. And that's the way she thinks of herself." And, of course, that is the point: millions of Americans with brown skin think of themselves as citizens, not illegals, who must prove their innocence.

From El Paso west, the boundary line with Mexico runs across a desert. It's another one thousand miles to the Pacific Ocean and San Diego.

San Diego County has more illegal immigration than any other area of the world. The county comprises but 3.3 percent of the 2,000 mile border front to Mexico; yet it accounts for more than 40 percent of the total apprehension of illegal aliens along the southern United States border and 25 percent of all apprehensions in the entire nation.

At the San Ysidro Border Patrol station near San Diego, I find that every agent wants to talk about his job. They seem to need to take time from their busy work schedules to put into words the paradoxes they encounter, perhaps to better understand them themselves. Winford Baze, one of the men who runs the San Ysidro station, is no exception. Baze is from my home town of Lubbock, Texas, where he played football for the Red Raiders. He tells me agents in his sector, which goes up to San Luis Obispo on the coast, arrest forty thousand illegals a month. In the Chula Vista area proper, a ten-mile stretch, they apprehend twenty thousand a month. The figures have escalated every year for the past ten years.

"In the past, when Mexicans came primarily to work in agriculture, they came from certain agricultural areas of Mexico," Baze relates. "Today they come from all parts of Mexico. They go into the metropolitan areas and take any job they can find. They blend in, just get lost in the city."

The next day I accompany Patrolman H.R. Williams on his mission to catch illegals. He is in his late forties, with brown hair, and a deep, soft, often-sad voice. He reminds me of those saddened by what they have seen in wars.

Williams and I drive to an area six miles west of the Port of Entry and near the Pacific Ocean. "This is a state park now, but there's a plan to take the fence down entirely and to make an international park out of it," Williams says. "Just on top of the hill newspaper photographers took pictures of Mrs. Nixon removing the fence as a Good Neighbor gesture—this was to indicate we would have an open border with Mexico."

He points out that the United States maintains a chain link fence only 26.9 miles along our 2,000 mile border. The San Diego suburb of San Ysidro has 3.6 miles of fence; Calexico has 5.5 miles of fence; Andrade, a quarter mile of fence. Six towns in Arizona have a total of 10.44 miles of fence. All of New Mexico has only one mile of fence—at Columbus. And El Paso has 6.12 miles of fence.

Otherwise, the border is open.

Williams points now to a four-strand barbed-wire fence that serves as a boundary between the United States and Mexico, saying, "It's down in most places." The Border Patrol hires a man who does nothing but repair the 3.6 miles of fence in the San Ysidro area. "And it's a full-time job."

Williams does not know if the plan will materialize to turn the state park into an international park, with people allowed to come and go freely. "But the state is going ahead and doing quite a bit of construction. They intend to open the park 24 hours a day, and when that happens we're in for some drastic problems. We have a real bad time controlling this particular area the way it is. A park will create problems for us that I'm afraid will be out of hand before too long."

We drive to the Pacific Ocean, the end of the 2,000-mile

border. "You see that on the beach the fence is only a small cable, set in poles about two-feet high. That's all there is between them and us. If we don't station somebody here they just keep moving north up the beach. At night this area goes completely wild."

There has never been such a mass exodus of people from one nation to another in the history of the world— short of war. I'm amazed, I comment to Williams, that it's not an open war.

"These people have a totally different attitude," he tells me. "To be able to work with them you need to be able to understand their attitude. They firmly believe that they have the right to be here, that with the Treaty of Guadalupe we took Texas and California and Arizona and some other properties. They feel that treaty is invalid and that they have the right to be here.

"You have to understand this about them, and work at it from that angle. Because if you approach them from the attitude that as far as the law is concerned they are wrong, they are an extremely hard-headed people. Once they decide they won't talk to you, they can be pretty tough to deal with. But if you sort of let them believe you accept their premise, that they are not historically illegal, they'll loosen up and talk to you. In this manner we manage to break quite a few of them."

Formerly, he said, they dealt with older people who wanted only to get a job and earn some money. "They never intended to cause anybody any trouble. They had knocked around a good many years and were interesting to talk to. Their way of life has been altogether different from ours. It's not uncommon to run into older men who don't read or write. It used to be a common thing to find those who had never ridden in a car. Some of the things they talk about as just everyday occurrences we would consider great hardships.

"But today you're dealing with a younger generation and their attitude, their thoughts are different. They've grown up with the idea that this is a land of milk and honey and they have the right to be here, and they're out to make their mark. These newer ones have a hostile attitude."

Violence has resulted, he continues, with several officers hurt. "In one instance, Agent James Bradshaw was scouting for illegals and three broke out on the mesa area. He and two other officers took off on foot after them. The aliens dropped over the edge of the mesa, out of sight. And Bradshaw, figuring they had kept running, went over the edge after them. One of them was waiting with a rock and hit him square in the forehead. Almost killed him. He's fortunate to be alive."

Williams and I drive through River Bottom, where Burriaga and I made the crossing from Tijuana—running and stumbling in the darkness, past *la migra*. How different it is now beside an agent.

"This River Bottom requires somebody in the area 24 hours of the day," Williams comments. "They jump a fence in Tijuana, get over to this side, come through this River Bottom and cross the freeway. Then maybe they'll catch a city bus that runs from San Ysidro into Chula Vista and on to San Diego."

We go over bumps. "It's rough. ..." Then: "This particular building is the Customs checkpoint area where they send most of the trucks through on this side, rather than flood the port." As he talks, I relive my experience of hiding with Burriaga in one of the trucks that had been cleared by Customs.

For the most part, Williams says, agents arrest illegals, write them up, then take them across the border. The majority are sent right back to Tijuana. "We use buses to take them from our office to the border, then walk them across the Port of Entry. They're willing to accept the fact that they've been caught But they'll keep trying until eventually they find a place where we're not watching, and away they go."

I have seen men in jails who weep over their sentences, and many, I remind Williams, wind up in federal prisons.

"Yes," he replies, "there are a few who wind up that way, smugglers and those with prior records."

What percentage of those apprehended, I ask, are sent from here to a jail or the El Centro Detention Camp?

"Apprehensions run eight hundred to a thousand in a 24-hour period," he replies. "Probably 20 to 30 of those are sent to El Centro. The others are run through the holding center here and then back to Tijuana."

Williams estimates that in California alone "there are four to five million illegals. There's probably a million and a half in Los Angeles and it's going to be two million. There's probably 18 to 20 million in the United States."

Later, at their San Ysidro headquarters, I sit with a group of Border Patrol agents. "Most of the robberies occur east of Spring Canyon, in Dead Man's Canyon. Even at 11 o'clock in the morning there are robberies and rapes there," says D.S. Hankin, who has been with the Border Patrol for 11 years. He says aliens "infiltrate" with legal workers who cross the border every morning to go to work. They know the Border Patrol does not have enough manpower to check everyone.

"The legal aliens have a staging area where contractors with buses and vans go to pick up their crews. The commuters come to this area and wait to be picked up. And the illegals, if they can mix with them, go out with the crews also, or get lost in the mass."

Another of the agents, J.H. Schwartz, relates that at five o'clock one morning, he was heading southbound on Interstate 5, about a quarter mile from the Port of Entry. "I had a busload of illegals I was taking back to Mexico, and I had to make a panic stop on the freeway to keep from running over about 50 wets who were dashing across the freeway from Mexico into this country." His point was that 50 more enter every time they return 50.

"The Border Patrol is very unpopular with certain employers," a woman agent, Chris Davis, tells me. Once in Yakima, Washington, the Immigration made a sweep in the apple and cherry orchards and returned six hundred illegal aliens to Mexico. "The next night we were catching all these aliens and they all had bus tickets. When we'd ask, Where are you going? they'd say, Back to Yakima. We sent them back to Mexico—again."

Bob Ritzdorf, a 20-year-old veteran on detail from Shelby, Montana, agrees that the Border Patrol is unpopular with some employers. "They don't like to see the Border Patrol come up and cart off 90 percent of their crew by arresting the illegal aliens." In 1977 he and another agent went on a check of field hands in Idaho. "There was no harvesting going on, but still we arrested 350 illegals. That just shows you the big increase in Mexican entries, and shows how they are spread out."

"Once, in the San Ysidro area, we had reports there were aliens in various rooms of a motel," one agent comments.

"We didn't know which rooms they were in, so we went around and we sniffed 'em out. Because there's a certain smell. *They stink*, because they don't take baths." Perhaps my face registers surprise at his blanket indictment of Mexicans. He tries to amend his sentiments: "Those people live like we probably did in the last century. I can remember when I was a kid, you didn't take a bath every day, you took baths on Saturday night. Those people don't have places to take baths, and they get to stinkin'. You ought to smell one of 'em who has been herdin' goats for about nine months. You ought to get one of his kind in the car on a wintry night when you've got to keep the windows up."

Mentally, listening to the Border Patrolmen, who seem to equate cleanliness with godliness, I recall the times I had run, frightened and perspiring, from such patrolmen

as those around me now. Should they have captured me I
know they would have thought I, also, was dirty and
smelled bad.

Back in Washington, D.C., I talked with Leonel Cas-
tillo, the Mexican American appointed by President
Carter to head the Immigration and Naturalization
Service.

"I am trying to change INS—make it humane and
effective, or as humane and effective and decent as we
can," he said. "Where someone says they're beaten or
abused or harassed or mistreated, I would like to look into
it so that I could at least know what is wrong and correct
it. I'm going to find some way to systematically investigate every instance that is reported, or as many on which
we can get anything substantive." Castillo attempts to
personally investigate every report of a Mexican national
who claims he is beaten or abused by Border Patrolmen.

"Our treatment of Mexican nationals has decidedly
changed," he continued. "We have a whole new group of
leadership in the Border Patrol—we have added a lot of
what I call 'Human Rights.' " He compared the Border
Patrol with the police in Houston, the city he came from.
"More Border Patrolmen speak Spanish and are of
Mexican descent," he said. "Some of those individuals are
beginning to show up in supervisory capacities. It's not
uncommon for them to come in and tell me they had to
give their lunch to the aliens because the aliens had no
money for lunch." Thirty percent of new Border Patrolmen, he added, have Spanish surnames.

His point, he said, was that Mexican American Border
Patrolmen will have a deeper understanding and sympathy for Mexican prisoners than Anglos. But I was not
sure. I later learned that the mother of one San Diego
patrolman I talked with was Mexican. And he was more
hostile than others toward Mexicans.

"Every wetback you pick up has beer on his breath and
two packs of cigarettes in his shirt pocket," this patrolman—who now is in a supervisory position—told me. "If
he has any money he spends it on beer, cigarettes, and
food—in that order." And, he added, "His women have to
fend for themselves."

VIII

The Losers

Border Patrolmen guess they apprehend only one out of five illegals who enter this country. As former Immigration Commissioner Leonard Chapman once admitted, "The guy we apprehend has to be very unlucky indeed."

Let us imagine that you are a typical Mexican peasant without land or a job. You head north. You know the risk involved in getting across the frontier is nothing compared with the risk of not making the effort, of the slow, sure death in the morass of your Mexican poverty. Once you cross the border you have, under United States law, committed a criminal offense. This offense, in the category of a misdemeanor, is punishable by as much as six months imprisonment or a fine of up to $500 or both. Depending on your luck, you could be expelled to Mexico immediately or you could serve time behind bars and be officially deported.

However, if you are apprehended near the border and

have come to the United States solely to find work and have no prior immigration history showing aggravated immigration offenses—if, in short, you are what a Border Patrolman might call Ol' Joe Wet on his first trip north your chances are good that you will be given a voluntary return, V-R'd, as the Border Patrol puts it, in lieu of deportation. This means that they write down your name and other data, in English, hand you a form (you being the typical Mexican illegal can't read English) but an agent explains in Spanish: "Here, sign on this line. It says you are voluntarily departing to Mexico without questioning your right to remain here." And you sign the form.

In 90 percent of the cases, Mexican illegals apprehended here are merely sent back to Mexico. But that is because 90 percent of the apprehensions are right along the border, the majority of them within a ten-mile sector of San Diego. As one official explained, "It would be physically impossible to conduct formal deportation proceedings for each illegal entrant. Therefore, except in aggravated cases, voluntary departure is the only practicable and effective remedy to remove such illegal entrants."

Once the paperwork is finished at Border Patrol headquarters, in all probability you, along with 40 or 50 other illegals, will be transported forthwith by bus to a Port of Entry. An armed United States guard ushers you and the other illegals through a small gate, where he warns you in Spanish that if you are caught again trying to sneak across the border you will be punished. You nod noncommittally, walk a few steps, and you are back in Mexico.

You may return to the United States that same day. Or, you may wait awhile and try your luck at a different place along the border. Let us presume you make another crossing but again are arrested. You could be V-R'd back to Mexico, or you could be put in jail—any jail.

For instance, Otero Souza, 48, and Juvero Souza, 21, who are distantly related, told me they came over for the second time—swimming the river at Laredo. "We were walking down the road near Castroville. The highway patrol picked us up. They put us in a jail in San Antonio, and we were held there three months. There are many Mexicans from Mexico kept there."

The elder Sousa says he first came here "five or six years ago." Juvero says, "I first came when I was 15. And I was here 15 days and the first day I got a job they caught me." He returned later and worked in construction, making $2.50 an hour. He saved money to help his nine brothers and sisters and his parents and after six months, never being detected, he returned on his own to Mexico. This then was his second time to be apprehended.

"Now the judges are too hard," Otero Souza says. "They keep you in jail as much as six months. After you are in jail that long you are sent here, like we are." I visited with them in the Port Isabel Detention Center. They were awaiting an official deportation hearing. They did not know when it would be held.

Deportation means you come before a judge who will notify you of your illegal status and the breaking of the law and who determines whether you will be allowed to stay, given a voluntary departure, or officially deported. If you must leave, as is the case with most undocumented Mexicans, you will be told not to come to the United States again to work illegally, because if you are caught again you will be expected to serve your sentence.

I repeatedly asked Immigration officials: Who determines if an illegal will be V-R'd immediately or held for deportation? What are your guidelines for punishing one man and not another? What are your guidelines for giving one man a deportation hearing and not another? Over and over again, various officers in the field admitted that it was how they "felt" about a case. I put the question to Assistant Immigration Commissioner Robin

Clack in Washington. Is it the man in the field, the agent, who determines if an alien will be officially deported? "It is usually handled at the sector headquarters staff level. . . . They would recommend a warrant of arrest. The arresting officer may say, I *feel* this fellow has such and such a record and I recommend that he be held for deportation."

The word "feel" strikes me as unusual in this case. When I was a police reporter, I never heard a city policeman tell me, "We *feel* this fellow has an aggravated case history." The police knew how to determine his arrest record at once. The Immigration Service, however, does not keep such records. "We stopped fingerprinting in 1964," an official told me. "We had too many cases. We didn't have the time to keep fingerprinting them." I watched Border Patrolmen tediously write up case histories on long sheets of paper. Later in headquarters a secretary, if he or she finds time, will laboriously copy the data on file cards. Should an agent want to check on an illegal, he or she can go to the mountain of files and manually go through looking for a name, hoping the alien has not used an alias.

In the event that you are apprehended far from the border, the Immigration Service asks you if you can pay your way back to Mexico. If you say you can't pay, the United States government gives you a ticket; but if you say you can pay, you must do so. Raul Beltrán, 23, with whom I visited in the Brooklyn detention center, is an example. Beltrán, from the state of Puebla, came to New York in 1972 on a student visa. The visa, as its name implies, is given to a person who plans to study, and is good only while that person is a student. Beltrán got one merely by assuring the United States authorities that he did not need to work while here.

But in fact, he did need to work. And what kind of work had he sought?

"Any job," Beltrán replies.

Beltrán's first job was in one of New York's Lower East Side apartment buildings, "mopping floors." He earned less than a minimum wage, but never complained. It was still "good money" by his standards. Later, washing pots in a large restaurant, he overheard his boss saying that he could never find a jobless American who wanted to wash pots, that the blacks and the whites "pick and choose" their jobs. He worked at one job and then another, often a daytime job and a nighttime job. "I never had any problems in three years. Then I went back to Mexico on my own," Beltrán says.

He crossed the border again for *el norte* in 1977 and was apprehended soon after his arrival in New York.

Beltrán proudly tells Immigration officials they do not need to pay his way back to Mexico. He will buy his own ticket. He has $300 he has saved from his time here before, when he washed pots and mopped floors.

It hardly seems right that he punishes himself with his honesty. No one would know if he gave a different name. No one would know if he said he could not buy his own ticket. But of course he would know.

"I want a clean record," he says. He sees Immigration the way a simple child sees Heaven: If you act good, someone up there marks a star on your record. But in the case of *la migra*, it doesn't always work that way. Often the most honest wetbacks are those who serve the most time.

Authorities gave Beltrán an opportunity of avoiding the official deportation hearing, but others do not have that choice. In fiscal year 1976, there were 719,756 illegals permitted to depart voluntarily. Nineteen thousand were officially deported.

Once at the El Paso Detention Center, I interviewed a prisoner, Roberto Cruz Tejado, and then listened to a deportation hearing that was held for him. In my interview, Cruz told me, in Spanish, he was 26 and from the state of Guanajuato. He said he was not married and that his parents were no longer living.

"I'm the oldest. I have nine sisters, four brothers. They're looking to me. I was 16 when I first came. I came back and forth for next ten years. I was picked up too many times. Each time they put me back in Mexico, and I'd come back again. I was picked up every year or every other year, but with no definite pattern.

"In 1969 I was working in Waukegan, near Chicago, in a restaurant. I made $1.50 an hour and tips. I didn't know anything about English. Once the police stopped me and asked me for my papers. And they put me in jail and held me there for ten months. And then I was sent back to Mexico. And I came back. I came over and worked in Dallas and Fort Worth. I worked shingling roofs. With a good contract, and a big house, with no ornaments, just a plain roof, you can make $65 a day. I learned the trade there. It's very hard to put on a roof. You get very tired. You first put down black paper and then the wood and then the shingles. I had three different bosses. I never had any problems, they liked my work."

Later, the deportation hearing began. Roberto Cruz Tejado does not understand English, so the hearing was held in English and translated. The judge read a legal document, and I heard a jumble of convoluted jargon that lawyers call English. I cannot follow it and Cruz, who has had two years in school, seems even more confused. Judge William Winert, a former trial attorney, read a statement of the "Rights of a Citizen" to Cruz. It was translated into Spanish. The judge asked Cruz if he understood it.

He demanded: "Answer Yes or No."

Cruz answered in Spanish: "I came here to work."

Exasperated, the judge repeated: "Answer Yes or No."

The translator repeated: *"Sí o no."*

Cruz nodded his head affirmatively.

The judge demanded: "You must speak! Yes or No!"

Cruz replied: "*Sí*."

Judge Winert looked at me, seated toward the back of the room, his face appealing for sympathy: "An order has come down. We are no longer to use the word 'illegal alien' but rather—and his tone turns sardonic—'undocumented worker.' They *are* here illegally, you know, it's a national disgrace!"

He seemed incapable of pronouncing "undocumented worker," however, and he continued to refer to Cruz as an "illegal alien."

The hearing droned on, and the judge exploded: "I hate the way this paper has been typed! Counterfeit is misspelled twice! I need to take off a day of my time to give spelling lessons, at the second grade level."

Cruz sank lower in his chair, apparently believing the outburst was directed at him.

The judge, however, was immersed in *his* problems: "I'm getting a headache over this spelling!"

Cruz' head dropped lower on his chest, not understanding the English, only the tones and gestures.

"It's been so bad today! God Almighty!" said the judge.

He played back the tape of the hearing, so the interpreter could repeat it word for word.

After nearly an hour, the judge asked Cruz: "Now is that clear? Do you understand that?"

Cruz replied in Spanish: "All I want to do is get out of here."

An hour later, it ended. Cruz was ordered deported to Mexico. He rose and said a polite "Gracias" to the woman interpreter, and "Gracias" to the judge. The judge did not seem to see him.

I walked over to tell Cruz goodbye and asked if he had understood any of the hearing. "No," he answered in Spanish, "*nada*." The entire hearing, I had supposed, was to tell him he had the right to protest his deportation.

"Oh, I go back, I never argue," he replied. Then he added: "I need to be out of this room, I could not understand the judge, the English or the Spanish. It gives me a pain in the head."

Leaving the room, I realized that our deportation hearings serve no purpose save to convince us we are being fair and following the law. We pay about $1.8 million annually to 45 Immigration judges to run through a ritual that only they understand. The hearing serves no purpose for a poor, unschooled man such as Cruz. We follow the letter of the law, but not the spirit of that law, which is justice and mercy. A man who understands none of the gibberish being shouted at him has received neither justice nor mercy. Sitting there for an hour was part of the punishment.

Let us continue to presume that you are the illegal, someone like Cruz. Should you again cross illegally into the United States, after you have been officially deported, you will have committed a felony. You could now be punished by as much as two years in prison, a fine of as much as $1,000, or both. Now, what do you do if you are the jobless Mexican? Before, you had always come over on your own, alone or with two or three buddies.

Now that the stakes are higher if you are caught, you turn to a guide or *coyote* to get you across. You go to Tijuana, join a group. You learn the groups there most always move at night, hoping to avoid detection. You walk from the heavily congested Mexican slum *barrio* of Colonia Libertad, where nearly a half million people are crowded on top of one another, and you climb through a broken fence and immediately you are in an area as large as the slum *barrio* but with no people—save for illegal immigrants, bandits, *la migra*, and the police.

This wasteland, U.S.A., is a battlefield. If you have a gun you are there to fight; if you are an illegal immigrant, you stay as inconspicuous as possible. You crouch, running over hills, through gullies, stumbling over hard, prickly, scrub brush. Suddenly a giant flying machine descends like some angry god. You fall face down. Lights flood the darkness and the noise of the engine over-whelms you. You have been in the United States before and know the machine is a helicopter, but others, crossing for the first time, are momentarily paralyzed by fear, the blinding light, and the deafening roar. You and the others are pinned down by the whirling blades of the helicopter. Eventually it lifts.

A gringo voice shouts in Spanish "Get up! Hands behind your head!" You move in the direction of a flashlight. You see an armed guard towering over you. He is one. And you are a group of 35. But you stay quiet, passive. It is part of your Mexican Indian survival technique to become as so much putty in his hands. He lines you up caterpillar style. "Empty your pockets!" You follow commands. It's a drill you've learned by heart.

"Now the writing starts," you perhaps will whisper to the initiate. The agent stands by the headlights of his vehicle, his questionnaires in hand. One illegal, wishing to be helpful, holds his flashlight.

"Name?" he asks in Spanish. And you may tell him your name is José Enrique Santarriaga Vivanco. Having studied Spanish the agent knows that Vivanco is the name of your mother and Santarriaga your surname. But the agent must ask: "How do you spell Santarriaga?" You accept his pen and write it out for him. That might be your real name or a name you have chosen for this particular crossing. However, if you are a typical Mexican you are loathe to lie about your name. No matter your poverty, you have been taught to be proud of your name, and negating it is like selling your birthright.

"Where were you born?" the agent asks. You may have been born in some remote village named by your Indian forebears. Again the agent likely must ask: "How do you spell that?"

"H-u-i-r-z-i-t-z-i-l-a-n," you may tell him. That is, presuming you are one of the lucky ones in Mexico who has gone to school and learned to spell.

Next the agent asks: "Is this your first time to enter the United States?" You may claim that it is. Or, you may choose to tell the truth.

Meanwhile a bus arrives and you travel to headquarters. You likely will now be transferred to El Centro Detention Camp and held there, awaiting your fate. You could be set free without a trial, or tried and sent to Leavenworth or another federal prison.

"We are the best customers for the federal prison system," one Immigration official boasted. So many Mexican illegals are now in our prisons that the federal Prison Bureau, which, like the Immigration and Naturalization Service is part of our Justice Department, separates them statistically from the other prisoners. As of January 1, 1978, the federal prisons held 29,380 prisoners, and of these 1,280 were being held after trial for immigration offenses. Half were on drug charges and the other half for smuggling aliens or being here illegally. Twelve wetbacks were in the prison at Leavenworth, Kansas—a maximum security institution.

The classification of Mexicans and Other Than Mexicans—OTM's they're called—is necessary, I was told, because the illegals go in and out so fast they lower the average time in prison for all prisoners.

"We keep a figure on the average time served by all federal prisoners," it was explained. "But so many Mexicans are sent to our prisons for relatively short periods that they were making the average time served by all prisoners look low." The average stay of Mexican illegals in a federal prison is five months. The average stay of the others is 15.8 months. The lower average for Mexicans, I was told, made the prison system look too lenient.

In addition to holding illegals in our federal prisons, as

well as in local jails or in the large Los Angeles and San Diego municipal correctional centers, we also hold them in four detention centers run by the Immigration Service. With the exception of the antiquated Brooklyn jail, the detention centers in El Centro, California, and in El Paso and Port Isabel, Texas, were built specifically for the incarceration of Mexicans. But other illegals also are sent to the centers, and in increasing numbers. I met many illegals from El Salvador, Peru, Colombia, Haiti, and a dozen different countries. When the jails were built, however, almost 100 percent of the illegals coming across the southern border were from Mexico. It was presumed in the early years of enforcing the immigration laws that we could apprehend all those crossing without documents at the border and jail them there.

Each center has facilities to process, house, and feed from 160 to 300 persons. Some illegals spend as little as four hours in the centers while being processed, and then are returned to Mexico. Others spend a few days. Others, particularly those to be deported or to be sent to a federal prison, may spend several weeks in a detention center.

Port Isabel, near Brownsville, on the Texas Gulf, is the oldest detention center.

"We get aliens from Oklahoma, Arkansas, Tennessee, Kentucky, Mississippi, Louisiana," Bob Cook, top man at the center, relates. A huge, ex-Marine who served in Korea and the Pacific Islands in World War II, he adds: "We send a bus every day to Lake Charles, Louisiana, to get prisoners from New Orleans. And we send a bus every day to Round Rock, Texas, to get prisoners from San Antonio, Dallas, and Corpus Christi. . . . We average 160 prisoners; we overnighted 102 last night."

Later, the office manager, Joe Garza, a pleasant, relaxed Mexican American, explains that the first detention center was in McAllen and it was moved to Port Isabel in 1961. At that time, Immigration had its own ship. "We used to deport people by ships to Mexico and at that time we had a lot of women coming across. And these women were prostitutes. They'd let themselves be caught, so that they could be sent back by ship, and earn money on the way." Garza adds that the Immigration Service's southern border division got rid of its ships. "Also, we stopped booking women." The Brooklyn center is the only one with facilities for both men and women prisoners. Outside the New York area, women illegals are booked in city or county jails awaiting their release or sentencing to federal prisons.

At lunch, I wait in the prison cafeteria for the illegals. At 12:00 sharp, the men come single file into the cafeteria. They look wild with thirst and hunger—wild for freedom. I join their queue. I stand behind one young man, perhaps 16. His pants are threadbare, ragged. He barely manages to keep oversized, shabby shoes on his feet. He has bushy black curly hair and only one good eye. We move along. Each of us carries a steel tray. A mess hall cook ladles out soup in one tray compartment, rice and beans in another. The men file rapidly, silently, through the line. The business at hand is plainly to use every free moment getting food and eating it.

We sit on wooden benches, jammed closely together, before a long rectangular table. Each man greedily spoons in the food, devouring it as if he hadn't eaten for a week. I want to relax, to take time to learn names and histories, to see them and have them see me. But I do not seem to be among social beings. The human aspect seems submerged by defeat. A man before me looks toilworn, dazed, depleted. Yet an alert glint lingers in his eyes, giving an impression of a caged beast, warily searching a way out. I am the only woman among 100 men. Yet no one speaks. No one looks to either side. I hear only the clatter of steel spoons on steel trays and a greedy chewing and gulping of food. I smile, and introducing myself to the man next to me, explain that I am a writer. He continues chewing. After a gulp he asks, casually, "What are you in here for?" He sees me as one of them, without papers. I give up talking while he eats.

After lunch I begin interviewing the illegals one by one. Before releasing a prisoner from behind bars to come to a private office for the interview, Garza explains in detail that talking with me is a voluntary act on the Mexican's part. He can easily refuse, yet none does so.

One of the illegals who comes to the office to talk with me is the young man in the floppy shoes and tattered clothes. He is Remberto Ortiz Rulfo, 17, from Los Mochis in Sinoloa. Now, alone in a room with me, and with his appetite for food appeased, he gives me an engaging smile and I note his good left eye twinkling. He is eager to talk about himself, about his working on a construction job in Mexico City, where he lost his right eye. "We Mexicans work harder than gringos," he brags. He tells me he has been working in asparagus and tomato fields, and he adds, "The gringos don't like to work on the farm." His personality is quite different now that he is away from the guards. He accepts me as someone he can trust, someone who is not employed or associated with *la migra*.

The illegals I interview are men who like hard work and who think that their only handicap in life is not to have the opportunity for it. They all tell me they came here simply to work, not to become citizens. They are that simple. Unlike others who imagine many roads to happiness, the Mexican illegal sees only one path: work. Adversities have a way of making men out of boys, and it is interesting for me to hear slightly built young men, such as Ortiz, who is no larger than most 12-year-old Anglo boys, tell me of working in construction or in factories, lifting 150-pound boxes. He will, apparently, try nearly any task that requires strength and endurance and is confident he can handle it.

Most of the Mexican illegals with whom I talked were from 17 to 45 years old. Several told me they made their first crossing when they were 13, 14, or 15. Jeronimo Serguro from San Luís de la Paz in Guanajuato is an example. He first came here when he was 13, crossing the river at Via Acuña into Del Rio with six companions. "I was here a year and eight months, working in San Antonio in construction. I began at $2 an hour, and made as much as $2.75 an hour. I was never caught by *la migra*. Then I heard my mother was dying, and I returned to see her. I went by bus. I stayed there in Mexico two years. My mother got well. And I came again to *los estados* in December 1976. I crossed over at El Paso and was caught and sent back. On January 3, 1977, I came back and got to San Antonio. They caught me in May, 1977, and sent me back to Mexico, but I returned. This is the fifth time." Serguro, who is five feet three and weighs 120 pounds, boasts the same as Ortiz: that he can work longer and harder than the Anglos. Some employers seem to agree. They replied to a *Los Angeles Times* survey that they preferred Mexican labor not only because it was cheap but because "Mexicans work harder."

Enrique Varela, a nonstop Cantinflas-type talker, told me he first came across the border when he was 15. He went to Oregon and trimmed apple and pear trees and picked cherries earning $1.60 an hour. "From Portland I went to Florida. I had nothing to eat for days, maybe a week, because I was afraid to get off the bus. Sometimes I had to, when the driver would signal me they were cleaning the bus. I was afraid if Immigration caught me the bus would continue without me." Sure enough, that happened. And he was arrested. But the Immigration officer felt sorry for him and gave him a pass good for a month.

In Florida, he started picking oranges. "I like to work hard—and I worked so hard I was perspiring and my pass got wet. I put it out in the sun to dry and then when I got through work I was so tired I forgot about it and it rained and when I came back to the place it was not there. So I stayed around until the work was ended and then returned voluntarily to Mexico."

His statement pinpoints another characteristic of the illegals: They are not really immigrant. Other immigrants who come great distances across oceans—as those from Europe, the Middle East, Russia, or the Far East—cut their ties and come to settle here permanently. But the Mexican travels to *el norte* over a land route or over an easily fordable river—and he goes and comes from Mexico as the Anglo travels from one state to another.

Priscila Anguilar, a mother of five, behind bars in a Brooklyn jail after she was arrested in an Immigration Service raid at the Newark factory where she worked, was the only illegal with whom I talked who said she had been in the United States for seven years. The others said they had been here less than a day up to a year or two years when they were arrested and deported. If they were not apprehended, they got homesick after six months to two years and returned on their own to Mexico for a visit that might extend from a month to many years. In most instances, it seemed to me, the Mexican generally does not consider a trip to *el norte* to mean he or she is leaving Mexico and their family for good. They do not bring their families with them because they often need to move fast, always hiding from the police and never sure of a job. Meanwhile their families can live more cheaply in Mexico awaiting the money orders.

Few have spent much time in a classroom. Of those I interviewed, the average was two to four years. Daniel Valdéz, for example, who has the innocent face of a hard-working farmer, was orphaned as a child and went to school only a couple of months. "I can only write my name," he said. His companion, 17-year-old Americo Barreda, on the other hand, had gone to school for six

years. His alert eyes and manner of talking convinced me
that given the opportunities he could achieve almost any
goal.

Each illegal repeats a refrain: "I am not a criminal. I
haven't stolen anything. I didn't harm anyone. I didn't
rob anybody. I didn't kill anybody. I am the head of my
family. My mother is looking to me. My sisters and my
younger brothers are looking to me. Now I'm in jail and
can't help them."

Several men, when I asked if their wives or mothers
knew they were in jail, began to cry. "No," they said.
They thought they were here working, earning money to
buy them food and clothing. If their wives and mothers
were to know, the men said, they would be on their knees,
praying for their welfare.

All of the undocumented Mexicans indicated they were
humiliated by the symbols of authority whose meaning
suggested they were criminals. "I feel humiliated, beaten
down, trampled upon," Geraldo Muñoz, 38, from the state
of Puebla, who was being held in the Brooklyn Detention
Center, told me. A few guards treat him well, he said, but
the others "treat us like animals."

Women illegals are even more vulnerable to any armed
United States agent who would abuse or assault them.
Martha Elena Parra López reported she was raped in San
Ysidro, California, by a Border Patrolman. The patrol-
man, later identified as Kenneth Cocke, resigned and
paid her $5,000 in damages.

Martha Elena Parra López said she was stopped along
with two male companions by a Border Patrolman near
Tijuana. Her two companions were forced back into
Mexico. Then, she told authorities in a sworn statement:
"Once he had me in on the front seat of the patrol car, he
went back a few feet and then he ordered me to take my
brassiere and panties off. I told him no and he insisted.
He then got his flashlight and asked me again 'Take your

brassiere off. I want to see if they are real and also take your panties off so that I can see if you have concealed money or documents.' After a long struggle with this officer until my strength was out, he stripped me completely and violated me. He made a statement and said, 'I hope you do not have any disease.' He then told me to get dressed and to get out of the patrol car and go to my country. I want to state that due to the sexual abuse—rape—I started to bleed very badly. I called Mrs. Vera Leon the next morning and described what had happened to me and she immediately contacted Mr. Albert R. Garcia."

She saw Garcia, an immigration adviser, and he took her sworn statement on June 7, 1972. Later he told me:

"I was determined that this case be made a model, that the assaults and rapes should stop. But I couldn't get a D.A. to handle the case. You know the law likes to protect its own. Nevertheless I notified state and federal congressmen and put on the pressure for some kind of justice.

"I don't know how many Mexicans have suffered assault and rape by an armed officer and never had the courage to report it."

There's a more innocuous, yet insidious type of abuse: seeing persons as commodities. As an example: One day at the Port Isabel Detention Center, I was seated at the far end of the mess hall. Harold Brown, pleasant, with a southern voice joins me.

"I'm the only gunsmith in Immigration. I'm responsible for six thousand guns," he tells me.

The aliens are filing in, lining up cafeteria style and then, seated, greedily devouring their food. Brown sits across from me, facing the Mexicans. He studies the bedraggled aliens in their tattered rags. The difference between the Haves and the Have Nots strikes Brown:

"Notice the difference at the border," he says. "You see progress on our side and poverty on their side. It is the system of government. I think we ought to take over and give them all our system, they'd be grateful for it."

His eyes are focused on the sea of illegals:

"Wouldn't it be great to put these men in uniform and let them attack their countries? I bet they would be good fighters," he continues. "Yes, I think we ought to take all the countries down there."

Brown was the only Immigration employee I heard who openly suggested our taking over all the countries "down there" but one agent told me he thought we did the Mexicans a favor by putting them in our jails. Mexico, he said, was dirty and our jails were clean.

"Frequent offenders may be the luckiest of all, for they will spend brief periods in United States prisons where they live better than they did at home," he told me. "They are taught a trade and how to speak English. When they finally succeed in entering the United States undetected, they'll be in a position to get the better jobs and to avoid discovery. Even behind bars, they may earn $150 a month in the prison factory. Many haven't earned so much in a year!"

None of the prisoners with whom I talked, however, felt they were lucky to be behind bars.

I found this a prevalent theme: The illegal thinks of jail as part of his destiny for being poor. "They scold us constantly, they have no right to do that," Rodolfo Dávila, a prisoner in the Brooklyn jail, told me. "We came here because we were poor, but we do not expect to be treated like children. We know what we have done and are willing to take the penalty, but I don't want to be scolded. Also, why do they have to handcuff us? We are not criminals. If they have already detained us there is no need for handcuffs. Since we don't speak the language we have to keep quiet. This happens to all the illegals. We can't help it if we are poor."

The illegal perhaps makes it easier on himself or herself by this simple, childlike reasoning: One is in jail not because one is immoral or a criminal but because one is poor. They think—and all that I have seen bears out their logic—that the greater the amount of money one has the lesser the possibilities of being apprehended. With enough money one can pay a veteran smuggler with a record for safe deliveries to Chicago or New York. Or you can buy documents in the black market. You can wait in a Mexican border town until you can obtain a Border Crossing Card. Or you can get a passport and United States tourist visa with which you can enter the United States at any point. I saw hundreds of illegal Mexicans behind bars, and with two or three exceptions, none had money for bail or a lawyer.

One story I heard repeatedly from the illegals. They would get safely across the frontier, get a job, and the day they were to be paid the employer called the Border Patrol. They were carted off to jail. And the employer avoided paying them.

If a Mexican is here illegally and other Hispanos know this, they have been encouraged by our government to call and have the Mexican arrested. Starting in 1957, Immigration gave rewards from $1 to $100 to anyone who supplied information leading to the apprehension of an illegal. One Immigration official told the Washington *Star* that 90 percent of INS apprehensions in the cities were as a result of telephone reports on illegals.

Father Humberto Hermosa, who has been serving the Mexican American community in Salinas, California, for almost three decades as pastor of the Christ the King Roman Catholic Church, told a reporter: "The illegals suffer much here. I tell the people in my church: Please, if you know of illegals here, don't call the police. The police already are looking.... Don't you be the one to report them."

Guillermo De la Sota, 26, of the state of Michoacán is an example of an illegal who was turned in by a Mexican American. "I spent four days crossing," he told me. "I had brought some cheese, tortillas, juices, and I began to walk through the hills until I got to Ramona, California. There I worked with a *ranchero*, tumbling down trees. He gave me enough to take the bus from Ramona to San Jacinto. From there I went through the hills to arrive in Perris. From there we, a friend and I, went over more hills, traversing embankments and lakes and other obstacles with coyotes all over us and then when we arrived near Long Beach the guards were checking people. But we passed unnoticed until we came to the freeway. We hitchhiked with a man who left us in Los Angeles. There we worked several days until there was no more work. There was not much to do, until we met this man, Basilia. I invited him to dinner and he said that he was in a hurry and left. Immediately after the Immigration caught us. Later I learned he has reported many illegals."

The average Mexican illegal with whom I talked seems naive, childlike, a peasant who has wandered into a big city. Many who come only to work may suddenly find themselves in totally new experiences, such as sitting aboard a luxury jet on a ride, courtesy of Uncle Sam.

Once I had accompanied the Port Isabel Detention Center office manager, Joe Garza, on an hour's flight from Harlingen to Houston. At the Houston airport, he took 35 illegals into custody, and we boarded a Southwest Airlines plane back to Harlingen. Neither the other passengers nor the stewardesses knew they had illegals among them.

I sat next to an illegal whose name I learned was Mauro Porras and who was 26, but I could not, try as I might, retain his attention more than three or four seconds. He had never seen an airplane except as one soared in the remote distance over his isolated village hidden behind the Sierra Madre range. Now he was being transported into the magical waves of the heavens, and all of this was some gift bestowed upon him, more thrilling than his wildest dreams. He might have walked

across a desert for six days and nights to gain entry into
this country. Perhaps on the high, windy plateau he
nearly froze to death at night and nearly smothered to
death in the heat of the desert sun. But whatever
hardships of hunger and thirst and other privations he
endured, this moment in the heavens—his glowing eyes
seemed to convey to me—made all of it worth the price of
admission.

His eyes riveted on the ample endowments of the tall—
about six feet—Texas stewardess, who was clad in mini-
attire that barely covered the here and there. Coffee?
Tea? A Scotch? She bent over Porras offering him her
brand of Texas hospitality. He and the others could not
speak English but accepted any given thing.

The stewardess, Garza said to me, obviously was brand
new on the job. He makes the trip every day, traveling
with about 35 illegals back to Port Isabel. "We'll write
them up and move them right on out." In the case of
those 75 or so who are bussed in daily from Round Rock,
"We'll give them a meal and by that night they'll be back
in Mexico."

The general plan for the past decade or more has been
to fill a bus at a detention center and send it to the
Mexican border. In the case of the Port Isabel center, the
bus would take the illegals to Brownsville and across to
Matamoros, where the illegals would be switched to a
Mexican bus line and told no one could get off until they
arrived in San Luís Potosí, a nine-hour bus trip with stops
only for fuel. These buses are chartered at United States
government expense. Besides San Luis Potosí, the Immigration Service also transports illegals to other destina-
tions such as Los Mochis and Chihuahua.

"This procedure raises a legal question in our mind,"
Julian Samora, a Notre Dame professor writes in his
book, *Los Mojados*. "Once an alien is in his own country,
what right does the United States have to force him into
the Mexican bus for a trip he may not want to take?"

The Immigration Service once allotted a couple of million dollars to a plan of flying Mexican illegals far into the interior of Mexico. The idea was to see how many would find their way back to *el norte*. I first learned about this plan in an accidental way. I happened to be flying to Mexico City in 1975. I flew from Washington, D.C., and changed planes in Dallas. I was waiting to board an American Airlines plane. Suddenly armed guards pushed aside the regular passengers to put a special group on board.

The special group looked as if they had just come from the brush: tattered work pants and shirts, worn shoes. No coats of any kind. "They came here without papers," one of the guards explained, adding they were now being flown back to Merida in the Yucatán at United States government expense. I asked if this were a common practice: "Oh sure," he replied "And it's costing the tax payers a lot of money."

After the illegals were seated, the rest of us boarded. We were soon airborne. I kept an eye on the illegals among us. At first, they looked abashed, intimidated, frightened. But once the stewardesses began serving them drinks and a choice of fish, poultry, or steaks, they began to smile, relax, and soon they seemed to be enjoying the flight more than the paying passengers.

However, while the Mexicans I saw seemed to be enjoying their free flight on American Airlines, the question that Professor Samora raised regarding our right to transport Mexicans within their own country remains unanswered. We can hardly imagine the equivalent happening to a United States citizen. Suppose you were a native New Yorker and Mexican authorities arrested you in Mexico City without your passport and arbitrarily transported you, as a means of punishment, to Alaska.

Both the United States and Mexico repeatedly have complained about the treatment of prisoners, but, neither—until 1977—had the leverage to force the other to make a prisoner exchange. The prisoners each country exchanged were for the most part drug offenders. The exchange permitted a prisoner to finish serving his term in his own country. No wetbacks were involved in the exchange.

Meanwhile, our prisons are jammed. Our courts are jammed. And the Immigration Service arrests increasing numbers of illegals and collects increasing mountains of statistics, but that's about all.

Only slightly more than one percent of all violaters are prosecuted.

For instance, in a three-month period in 1977, about 300,000 illegals crossed the United States-Mexico border, but in that same period only 3,351 were convicted.

Given this data, why are we doubling the Border Patrol? If we apprehended a million in 1977 is our goal to apprehend two million? To build more jails? To recycle more Mexican workers in and out of them? I asked El Paso Chief Agent Swancutt why we apprehended so many when the prosecution was about one percent. "We've got to show some force," he replied. "Otherwise it would be completely out of hand."

Agent Luckey in McAllen told me: "I think we are holding all these prisoners as hostages." He thought a moment and added: "We want Mexican oil, and we have a commodity with which to bargain to get it."

In my visit with Immigration Commissioner Castillo in Washington, D.C., he told me how he had tried to improve the treatment of illegals.

He said he began his changes by giving a new name for the four INS detention centers: "We now call them Service Processing Centers."

When he visited the Brooklyn center, he said, he found it "a miserable place. And I just told them: I'm going to close it. Find another place.

"We have a totally new and different approach," he continued. "We're using a minimum of Bureau of Prison standards. We're putting in television. I put in a library in Brooklyn, put in a recreational area, am putting in radio and music. We're going from double bunks to single.

"Our facilities have changed drastically, just drastically. I've put in money in the San Diego sector and I'm going to redo the El Paso center. I gave them $100,000. They have a soccer field coming up. A lot of things. I'm closing the Port Isabel center, and we will build somewhere else. I'm going to reduce the time the illegals spend in the centers."

Throughout my travels I was aware that Castillo's influence as head of *la migra* is being felt. But as he told me about his plans I thought of an interview I had earlier with an illegal. Again, I saw the tears in the eyes of this man as he spoke of his wife and the nine children who were dependent on him for food. He didn't come here to play soccer. He came here to send home a money order.

The presence of millions of brown people in our midst somehow never caught the nation's attention—although they are gradually changing the nation.

Forced to consider solutions to the presence of illegal Mexicans and other brown-skinned aliens, we will begin, more and more, to consider their history, their culture, and the totality of the impact of their lives on ours.

Hispanic people, representing 23 different nationalities, number an estimated 22 million in this country—documented and undocumented.

They are the nation's youngest and fastest growing group, and in a few years they will outnumber blacks as our largest minority.

Already their spiraling population has made the United States the fourth largest Spanish-speaking nation in the world. Spanish—the core of the Hispanic's culture and character—now ranks with Chinese, English, and Russian as one of the main world languages. And, if some projections are right, Spanish will be the language of the largest number of people in the Western world by the twenty-first century.

*Generally, we tend to think of the United States
Spanish-speaking as a regional people: Mexicans in the
Southwest, Puerto Ricans in the Northeast, particularly
New York, and Cubans in the Southeast. However, 1978
statistics show:*

*The state of New Jersey has more Hispanics than the
State of Arizona.*

*The state of Illinois—with more than one million
Spanish-speaking—has more Hispanics than New Mexico
and Arizona combined.*

*Of the three largest groups in the Hispanic category—
Mexicans, Puerto Ricans, and Cubans—only the Mexicans
have illegals among them.*

*Mexican Americans comprise an estimated 60 percent
of all United States Hispanics. Today one Texan out of
five is of Mexican origin. Mexicans add up to 98 percent
in some of the southern counties of the state.*

*The figures are even more impressive in California: Los
Angeles alone has 1.5 million Mexican Americans and
ranks after Mexico City as the second largest "Mexican"
city. It is predicted that before 1985 the Mexican Americans in California not only will be the minority—they
already are that—but the* majority *in that state.*

*Puerto Ricans, the second largest group of American
Hispanics, number 1.7 million on the mainland and 3.1
million on the island.*

*All Puerto Ricans, being United States citizens by
birth, can travel freely to and from the mainland. Many
work here for awhile, then return to the island. There's
now a reverse migration, with more Puerto Ricans
returning to the island than those coming to the mainland. (If Mexican workers are legalized, they, too, might
establish the same type of pattern as the Puerto Ricans.)*

*Cubans are the third largest Hispanic group. They
number about 750,000 and live for the most part in
Florida, with a heavy concentration in Miami.*

Before the Cubans arrived, Miami was one of our

typical, functional, steel-and-concrete cities that seemingly came from the same cookie-cutter press. Miami now pulsates with a latino rhythm. Just as the French gave New Orleans a distinctive flavor, so the Cubans have made Miami one of our distinctive United States cities.

Among United States Hispanics, "We Cubans are the best off—economically," Miguel Cabrera, who fled from Castro when he was 18, told me when I visited him and his family in Miami. And statistics bear him out. Cabrera does not think Cubans are endowed physically or mentally with greater attributes than other Hispanic people, but rather that they have suffered less discrimination in this country.

"I know I am lucky when I compare myself with millions of Mexicans who are picked up and deported—from what was once their own land. They have it rough."

He pointed out that a Mexican who swims the Rio Grande can be arrested and sent to prison, whereas a Cuban who swam the river would not be classified as an illegal—"he would be seen as a refugee, and welcomed here."

Because the Mexicans represent the largest number of Hispanic people in our midst, they naturally have the largest impact on our lives.

The Mexicans, to a larger degree than most immigrants, retain their traditions as well as their language. They constantly receive "new blood" from their home country. New immigrants come from small villages with deeply ingrained customs and with deep, personal, religious convictions. They come in many instances speaking only Spanish. In short, they always bring a bit of old Mexico to the Mexican Americans and help them in retaining a sense of their rich heritage.

The following chapters show how the Mexicans, legal and illegal, influence our lives and how they view this Promised Land.

IX

The Illegals
and the Church

Thoreau once reminded us that it is never too late to give up our prejudices, and churches often have provided the means of persuading us to escape from the fear of those who may be different.

Blacks moved themselves and the rest of us through Civil Rights largely by acting, at least in the beginning, through their Protestant churches. Martin Luther King, Jr. and others taught us to see black as beautiful.

In the same way, many of those in the Roman Catholic Church are among the nation's most powerful voices for equal justice for downtrodden brown people—those who are here both legally and illegally.

In its first official support for the political and social aspirations of this minority, the Catholic Church endorsed the grape boycott in 1969, lending its moral strength to César Chavez' fight to obtain better wages and working conditions for farm workers. When grape and lettuce boycotts became national issues, parishioners were urged in church bulletins and diocesan letters to help *la causa*.

Pablo Sedillo, a nephew of the Sedillo brothers with whom I visited in Las Vegas, New Mexico, is one of the nation's most powerful spokesmen for the cause of the illegals. Sedillo, who heads the Church's Secretariat of the Spanish Speaking, points out that Spanish-speaking people, the majority of them Mexicans, now are in all the 167 dioceses in the United States.

"We comprise one quarter of all the Catholic population in the United States. That's about twelve million people." He believes that 95 percent of the Chicano clergy "are very much involved with our people, experiencing their pains and tribulations every single day. And that's because they, too, have gone through privations and feel a closeness to our people."

In San Antonio, I sat for several hours with Catholic Sister Adela Arroya, immigration consultant for the Catholic Service for Immigrants as she listened to stories from Mexican illegals.

One illegal, Juana, works in a San Antonio beauty shop. She is 35, petite. Sister Adela helps her by translating letters from Spanish to English requesting legal working papers.

A laborer and his wife, who is holding a small child, come next. The couple is dressed in freshly washed clothes, smelling of soap. The infant has a brand new dress, including new baby shoes that appear to have been put on for the first time that morning. The father has fierce eyes, like those of an animal at bay. I note his sun-darkened skin, his calloused hands. He tries to understand the rules and endless documents the Sister tells him might one day make him legal. The child in the mother's arms already is legal. She was born here.

"The trouble," Sister Adela tells me later, "is that the illegal worker must prove he or she can make a certain amount of money. Then you have a greater possibility of convincing authorities you should stay here. The farm workers coming in today seldom can meet that requirement."

In many instances, the Church tries to persuade immigration authorities to grant legal status to immigrants. One instance, she said, was that of a Mexican mother whose sons had served in World War II, the Korean conflict, and the Vietnam War. "She was to be deported as an illegal," the sister said, "but we persuaded the authorities she should be recognized as legal."

In it's "Call to Action" conference in Detroit in October, 1977, the Catholic Church established its position on the illegals. One of the conference's resolutions called for "Amnesty for undocumented immigrants whose departure from the United States would impose upon them or their families *any* hardship." It also asked for "implementation of a statute of limitation to the Immigration and Naturalization Act provisions ... so that those who have developed standing and work in the community may no longer be perpetually vulnerable to deportation."

The conference also mandated the Church "to seek an end to the abuse of human and civil rights of undocumented immigrants ... through Immigration and Naturalization Service enforcement tactics." And it called for the Church to "Publicly support its teaching that a worker has the right to seek employment anywhere in the world."

The resolutions of the conference supported the exposure of "U.S. multi-nationals' economic interest in Latin America ... which cause [the immigration] of economic refugees into this country."

By bringing into the picture the multinational corporations and their effect on the immigration of Latinos to the United States, the Catholic Church's position indicates the United States—as the home base for most of these corporations—bears a large responsibility for the presence here of illegals.

The Church calls for economic aid to Latin America, particularly Mexico, to alleviate some of the conditions that feed this immigration to the United States.

Through the years the Church has emphasized that if employment opportunities were available in the home country, the prospect of temporary jobs in the United States would attract few workers.

Reverend Juan Hurtado from San Diego has stressed the role of the Church in helping the poor, the powerless, the voiceless, the oppressed.

"The Church must authentically reflect a liberating crusade. It must support the Chicanos in their cause of religious, social, educational, political and economic betterment," he has written.

A Ph.D., Hurtado is perhaps the most vocal of the leaders calling for change within the Anglo-dominated Church. To change institutions and discriminatory customs, he says, the Hispanic people themselves must change "from meekness and passivity to organized strength and agressivity. We must apply pressure from a base of power."

In the late 1960s a group of activist Chicano priests formed such a base of power. This group became known as PADRES, Priests Associated for the Religious, Educational and Social Rights of the Spanish-speaking in the United States. "We realized that the people felt alienated from the Church. The Church was not reaching the vast majority of Chicanos and other Spanish-speaking Catholics." In 1970 PADRES held its first convention and officially stated: "The American Church is desperately in need of a conversion to the ideal of the poor Christ who was committed to justice for the poor and who constantly insisted that those who have human and material resources ought to use these in favor of the dispossessed."

In 1971 at their Second National Congress PADRES protested to the United States Catholic hierarchy:

"The United States of American and the United States of Mexico are awakening to the phenomenon of the existence of a distinct and emerging ethnic group, the Mexican American, the Chicano.

"The Church has failed to defend the social and economic justice of our people. It has done the opposite by remaining silent without giving any support to our struggle for an ideal justice.

"PADRES must continue to work with our people to obtain liberation from all oppression including structural dependency imposed by various institutions. These institutions from the social to the academic level have blatantly, although maybe inadvertently, discriminated against us. The Chicano in the Church should not continue in a missionary status."

As a result of intensified pressures brought by PADRES and other groups, the United States Catholic Church in 1970 named the first Mexican American auxiliary bishop, Patricio F. Flores of San Antonio. Other appointments followed: Juan A. Arzube, Auxiliary Bishop of Los Angeles (1971); Rene H. Gracida, Bishop of Pensacola-Tallahassee (1972); Gilbert E. Chavez, Auxiliary Bishop of San Diego (1974); Robert F. Sánchez, Archbishop of Santa Fe (1974); Raymundo Peña, Auxiliary Bishop of San Antonio (1976); and Manuel Moreno, Auxiliary Bishop of Los Angeles (1976).

Hurtado says, "Hispanic priests and other Spanish-speaking clergy should be promoted as bishops in all those dioceses in which at least 50 percent of the Catholic population is Spanish-speaking and be further entrusted with jurisdiction over all the Spanish-speaking in their areas."

In San Antonio, I visited with Catholic priests and nuns at the Mexican American Cultural Center, which I see as a training place for the new leadership developing among Mexican people. The center is a combination school and church and home, spread over a large campus.

I visited with the center's associate director, Ricardo Ramírez, a priest, who told me he grew up—in a white-oriented society—"as a brown-skinned Chicano."

What, I ask, is his definition of a Chicano?

"A Mexican American who protests the injustices that we as a race have suffered," he replies. He explains that the word is thought to have originated in Mexico, probably in the northern state of Chihuahua. It was used in this country beginning in the 1930s as a term Mexican Americans gave themselves to indicate a status that was neither entirely Mexican nor entirely United States American. "Then it came into general popularity in the 1960s, with the protest movement," Ramírez continues.

"Just as the Negroes needed to recognize their blackness, we needed to recognize our Indianness. For centuries we had been saying: We are pure Spanish people. Now we say we are Chicanos, a separate and distinct race. We are for the most part Indian. We have for the most part brown skin. We have the problems of being told by others that we are inferior. Now we are demanding our human rights." He points out no one pays attention unless you are organized, unless you have the lever to force a change. "We are learning from the blacks how to organize. But we are at least a decade behind. However, we are starting as the blacks did, in our churches. Here our real leaders likely will emerge."

Throughout its history, until the present time, the United States Catholic Church did nothing to help or encourage Mexican Americans to train as leaders.

"At the seminary I was in houses where I was the only Mexican American, and the only person who spoke Spanish," Ramírez recalls. He had to adjust to Catholic schools that were created for Anglos who dressed, thought, and spoke like other Anglos, "They knew nothing about my language, the kind of food I might like, or the books I might enjoy. Nothing about my heritage, traditions, interests." He adds that since they could not understand him, "They tended to see me as an outsider, a 'foreigner.' "

To explain why it is deeply ingrained within the United States Catholic hierarchy to view the Hispanic as an outsider, Ramírez goes back in history: The Spaniards in the fifteenth century brought the Catholic religion to the Americas. In the United States portion of the Americas they left the faith but not the hierarchy. "In this country, it's been imported for the most part from Ireland." For centuries now it has remained a hierarchy dominated by Anglos. He points out that just as the blacks in this country were kept out of white Protestant churches, the Hispanic people often were sent to separate Catholic churches, or told to sit at the back. He says many Mexican Americans have seen church signs: "Mexicans not allowed," or, "The last four benches reserved for Mexicans."

The new Chicano clergy are changing the concept of the Church: moving it from its emphasis on dogma and donations to a servanthood for the needy. Most Mexicans, they realize, are poor. It is to them they direct their attention. A large, dynamic, yet soft-spoken Jesuit priest, Edmundo Rodriguez, is an example. Seeing him going about his tasks in San Antonio, I think of a Miguel Unamuno phrase about a beloved Catholic priest who was an "everyday" person among his people, as common as the bread they ate, and as necessary to their lives.

His parish is a square mile in size and, with the exception of one Italian family and a few blacks, all of the people are Mexicans, documented and undocumented. "The area has been one of high transition," he says. "I figure that about one-third to one-half of the parish would turn over every year. When you're talking about twelve to fourteen thousand people, that's five thousand new people coming in and five thousand people moving out."

Rather than a center for doles to the poor, he sees his church as "a center for social-political action." And he moves to create power for the poor, having learned his methods from Saul Alinsky, whose organizing skill involves the creation of power bases to develop autonomy in poor neighborhoods. As an example, Alinsky once recalled visiting a Catholic priest in a poor, powerless neighborhood. "Your people are unemployed, their families are shot to hell and you're not doing a God damn thing about it," he told the priest. "You sit on your ass in the sacristy. You want to be a leader? Get with your people, get out in the streets and fight for the union.... The enemy is low wages."

Rodriguez, having studied Alinsky like a text, put together a sponsoring committee and money that formed COPS, Communities Organized for Public Service. With 30 people, he helped create an organization now boasting more than five thousand members. "My role is to get others started, to push others into doing what they are capable of doing. For instance, there's a school board election. We push the school district, they deputize their prinicipals and assistant principals to register people to vote, and this makes it convenient for parents to go to the school and get registered." Now, with many people involved, there is an urgency on the part of the community to vote. People have a sense of "Well, I better get registered if I am to participate."

Members of COPS initially rallied around a simple issue: Their children had to walk over a railroad trestle to get to school. "For about ten years people were talking about putting up a pedestrian bridge across that ravine. Our people began to get angry because what seemed an obvious solution, and one that didn't require a lot of money, was resisted."

Then, Rodriguez continues, "We came to see that a small number of people without a lot of information and without constant agitation would not be successful in getting much of anything, so that helped to organize more people. We had a lot of people pushing the school board and eventually what came out of it was not a pedestrian bridge but a whole new school. This was approved by the school board, on a top priority basis. When I look back I think it was good we didn't concede right away because we would have had a pedestrian bridge."

He hopes through COPS to break up the at-large elections into districts. "This will give people in a smaller area a chance to get elected by doing shoe leather work and handshaking, getting to know people." It will, in short, bring city government back to the grassroots level where people can make their leaders more responsive to their needs.

In Chicago's west side, another Mexican American priest, David Gallegos, lives among the poor—legal and illegal—offering them a servanthood.

I find a warmth and comfort in his old three-story house, with wood-burning fireplace. Once abandoned and ready for demolition, Gallegos bought it for $5,000, then repaired it and named it "The Place."

Born in Belen, New Mexico, Father Gallegos, now in his late thirties, works six days a week as a social worker among alcoholics, drug addicts, the jobless, the homeless, and the illegals. Most of the people he serves, he says, "don't know that I am a priest—at least in the beginning." On the seventh day, as he puts it, "that's another whole life."

Gallegos, a member of the Serbite Order, spent his college years in Europe and the British Isles. After his ordination in Italy, he started working in the poor areas of Chicago. "I liked the work, I settled into it." His handsome face radiates the joy of one who feels he has been called to help others, and who has had the courage, talent, and patience to answer that call.

"There's a group we call West Town Community Youth Services," he relates. "We get calls from parents who say they are having problems with the kids, and we go out where they are. We don't have a counseling office, we have an office where phone calls come in. We started with five people. Once we got it started, we were able to get funds from the state, from the Department of Mental Health, and from the department of Child and Family Services of the City of Chicago. Now we have a paid staff of 48, including several social workers with college degrees.

"We hope to start an alcoholic treatment program, one that is completely different from anything else," he continues, pointing out that in the slums, "you need a variety of services, because the main problem is not any one thing, so much as it's everything. And even if you isolate any one problem you have the extreme of it."

Gallegos also plans to start a residential home for teenagers, "kids who have had some sort of court involvement. For various reasons they can't stay at home. The parents don't want them. Or in some instances they don't have homes. Their mother died, maybe their father killed her, and he winds up in jail, that sort of thing." He hopes to have The Place approved as a residential home for 12 to 16 young people.

His home is also a haven for those without papers. When I was staying at The Place, there was an illegal living on the floor above me. Millions of brown-skinned persons like Father Gallegos are helping those who want only a chance for a decent job. He and scores of other priests and nuns have told me it would not be Christian to turn from your door a hungry man, desperately striving to feed his family.

Gallegos says we must get to the causes of poverty and unemployment to solve the problem of the illegals.

Meanwhile, he says, we must be as "brothers" and "sisters" to them, granting them the same human rights that we say we want for others around the world.

Sedillo, the Catholic spokesman quoted earlier, pointed out to me that the Church long has had grave reservations regarding the penalties proposed for employers who hire undocumented workers. Sedillo says that a common employment identification card, to be carried by every worker, would provide the greatest protection against discrimination against minority groups in hiring practices. However, the Carter Administration has rejected proposals for such a card, and substituted a list of documents by which the job applicant may try to convince an employer he has a right to work and by which the employer can protect himself against a charge of violating the law should it turn out that the employee is indeed an undocumented alien.

Many of these documents, such as the Social Security card in its present form, can be easily counterfeited. Also, dishonest employers would have no difficulty in protecting themselves against prosecution by merely making a notation on each employment application that they have seen, for example, a United States birth certificate or a Social Security card.

"The Administration proposal is seriously deficient for its failure to make it mandatory that the employer require every job applicant, citizen and alien alike, to produce evidence of his lawful employability," Sedillo said. He added that it was not unreasonable to assume that only "one who does not look like an American" would be required to produce documentations. "Clearly the issue of discrimination in hiring practices has not been met."

Following President Carter's announcement in 1977 of his proposals on the undocumented alien, Bishop Thomas C. Kelly, the General Secretary of the Catholic Bishop's Conference, stated:

"President Carter's proposal on undocumented aliens is aimed at drastically reducing illegal immigration while at the same time providing relief for those currently residing in this country. It is a step in the right direction but one which requires much more development.

"The Catholic Bishops of the United States have long supported legislation which would grant a meaningful 'amnesty' to undocumented aliens and have opposed any punitive measures against them. Many of these persons have established families whose members include American citizens with all the rights of citizenship. To cut these families off from their meager economic sustenance and to force upon them the great hardship of emigrating or of family separation would be both inhumane and immoral.

"The positive approach which the President has taken to avoid such hardships, in his recognition of the human rights of the people involved and the responsibility which our government bears for their presence here, is most welcome. But the President's proposal grants permanent residence only to a small minority of undocumented aliens, those here since before 1970, while the great majority are granted only temporary relief. The heart of America is big enough to do more. . . .

"In attempting to prevent unlawful entries and sanctioning employers who knowingly hire such persons, every effort must be made to protect the civil rights of our citizenry and to avoid discrimination in hiring and employment practices, especially against Hispanic and other minority groups.

"President Carter is to be commended for recognizing a problem and attempting to solve it, but we urge an even more meaningful program to meet the needs of the human beings so vitally affected."

X

With the Farm Workers

Newly arrived immigrants from Mexico constantly are joining the migrant stream. Crew chiefs who hire field workers claim it is impossible for them to know who has legal documents. They say they are not trained to recognize false or counterfeit papers, and only an officer schooled in documents can tell an illegal from a legal immigrant accurately.

The Immigration agents, meanwhile, see any brown-skinned workers in a field as possible illegals. And they mount a strategy to capture them as in any war. They often launch predawn surprise assaults. They determine the disposition of vehicles, weapons, walkie-talkies, and air surveillance. And they count themselves successful if it's all over before the growers or the workers know what has hit them.

Workers, both legals as well as illegals, say they live in fear of the raids. They say they are intimidated by constant demands for proper identification.

I worked in fields alongside Mexican laborers in California and New York. I could see that the distinction another Anglo might make between a United States citizen and an illegal loses its significance among scores of brown-skinned, Spanish-speaking Mexicans picking tomatoes or clipping onions. Then it becomes a question of a people who see themselves as one, bound together by their poverty and caught up in a system in which they traditionally have had no bargaining power.

The illegal alien and the legal farm laborer both lose miserably in the fluctuation of our immigration laws. And nowhere is the ambivalence of our immigration policy so clearly seen as in the case of Mexican farm workers. For we are expelling them in one program and bringing them in as laborers in another.

In the 1977 harvest season, onion growers in the Big Bend area of Texas said a crisis existed—they could not find any Anglos to do the stoop labor. They said they had tried help-wanted ads in the newspapers, but no Anglos applied. They needed *Mexicans.*

The growers called on another Texan, House Majority Leader James C. Wright, and they went to the White House. The President and the House Majority Leader agreed: Don't let the onions and cantaloupes rot. Call in the Mexicans.

This was indeed to be a harvest of ironies. The Immigration Service reversed its policies. Agents issued work cards to eight hundred Mexicans permitting them to cross the border and harvest onions and cantaloupes in the border town of Presidio, population 1,295.

At the same time other Immigration agents were rounding up Mexicans and deporting them from the fields of upstate New York, New Jersey, and along the Eastern Shore.

In July 1977, at the peak of the season for tomatoes, cucumbers, and other crops, agents held a series of surprise raids on migrant labor camps along Maryland's

Eastern Shore. In the predawn, Immigration agents burst into the Irving Handy labor camp near Hurlock and arrested ten illegal aliens as they were piling onto trucks to go to the fields. The next morning agents raided the same camp again, arresting 28 more illegal workers who were jailed in Baltimore and eventually deported.

The grower, Irving Handy, said he lost his last crop of cucumbers because of the raid on his camp. "You can't hire workers at the last minute to go in after another crew to pick," he said. "I couldn't get anybody to pick it so I had to plow it under. It cost me $15,000."

Another grower, H. William Overholt of Pocomoke City, said the raids "could not have come at a worse time. Immigration officials just drove into my field and over the tomato crop. They had no warrant and they didn't contact me to tell me there would be a problem in my fields."

Overholt and other Eastern Shore growers contend the Mexican crews are the hardest workers they can hire. "They are industrious people," Overholt said. "But these raids on illegals are very disturbing to us. It is another black eye for the farmer. I don't willingly hire the illegals, but we need them—we need that stoop labor."

Robert Schmidt, the warden at the Brooklyn Detention Center, told me he gave agents a tip that led to other raids on New Jersey fields during the peak of the harvest in 1977.

"I drive to and from my home in New Jersey every day, and I pass fields with farm workers," Schmidt related. "Not many people realize it, but New Jersey is a large agricultural state. Forty percent is developed farm land, producing corn, apples, peaches, tomatoes, potatoes. So there is plenty of work for illegal aliens."

Schmidt saw brown-skinned workers in fields and surmised that some might be illegals. He tipped agents to investigate, and they made several raids, netting 279 illegals. Proud of his part in the arrests, Schmidt handed

me a New Jersey newspaper with headlines: "Harvest
Rots as U.S. Nets Alien Laborers."

"In South Jersey," the article began, "the fields are
lush with rotting tomatoes." It went on to say that 1977
had been a good year for the farmers until all their
pickers were taken away by Immigration agents.

Another grower, Warren Porch of Pedricktown, New
Jersey, described the arrest of his crew: "At 6:00 A.M., this
helicopter swooped down and four vans and three cars
filled up my front yard like it was a parking lot. They
never told me who they were. They treated me like dirt."

Of his field hands, Porch said, "The Mexicans really
worked. Others will not work as hard as they do. We're
supposed to hire welfare recipients who are legal. But the
truth is they just won't work." He said he has tried
employment agencies and newspaper advertising with no
luck. "I had five come out here to pick, and I found them
sitting in a car listening to the radio." Porch admitted
that he and his neighboring farmers have hired illegals
for years, and he added: "Everybody in this section has
some, and that's a fact."

Another grower, Benny Sorbello of Woodstown, New
Jersey, said that after his workers were jailed he and his
family worked feverishly to harvest his green pepper
crop. Most of the crop was lost, however, and he said that
at least $20,000 worth of tomatoes rotted in his fields.

Sorbello said he would hire anyone who wanted to
work—"I don't care who they are as long as they work."
But he added, "Mexicans are the only people I can find
who will do stoop labor." Of the Immigration agents, he
said: "They pulled my workers right out of the fields and
put them in their vans. I said to them 'What's gonna
happen to my crops?' And they said, 'That's your problem.' They jailed all my workers and those men had to sit
in prison for 21 days when they could have been picking
my crops."

The growers and the workers all suffer by the constant raids by Immigration agents, a Catholic priest, George B. Dyer of San Antonio, reports. Now on the teaching staff of the Mexican American Cultural Center, Dyer says that the raids keep the undocumented and the documented in a state of constant fear. "All migrants are oppressed." In many instances, he says, the migrants are no better off than the blacks of the pre-emancipation years. They don't always have a cabin or any semblance of security, and they are often still held as slaves.

The priest, a vibrant man in his 40s, reports he had been in some migrant camps where people have called him aside and whispered, "They're keeping me here against my will. I'm not being fed. Can you get me out of here?" There is a right-to-access law that says you may legally come and go into the migrant camps, "But workers are not allowed to do so."

Once the priest was held at gunpoint outside a camp in Virginia, not too far from Washington, D.C. "It was like entering a prison. I had to clearly state my business. So I got tough but it was a long while before he put the gun down." If a migrant steps out of line, "you find him in a ditch or a trench. People are actually shot. And the murders go unsolved."

Father Dyer has accompanied Texas field workers as they fan out to the East Coast, as well as to the Midwest, particularly around the Chicago area, and also to South Carolina, Virginia, Maryland, and Delaware. Mexicans comprise the large majority of this migrant stream. The other workers, for the most part Puerto Ricans and blacks, "tend to be more single people, more men than woman, and you see less children. They are more seasonal farm workers in a particular area. The Mexicans are usually families who travel together. You can go into the fields and see five- and six- and seven-year-old children, working a full day. The families are so poor they need the children to work in the fields just to make it. So for the most part the children don't get to go to school and become lawyers and change things."

A "humble, meek" Mexican worker who does not speak English or understand Anglo laws does not know how to make demands, to fight back. "If you put a gun up, he's going to turn away. He's not going to agitate, to show anger. Yet growers continue to use intimidation with threats to life. If a grower wants to deal with migrants in a discriminatory way, he does so.

"The use of terror and slavery are at the heart of the labor contract system," the priest continues. "Migrants travel across country at their own expense. Mothers also must work. And they must carry their babies from one area to another with changes of water and diet and they get sick and often there are no doctors to help them, as most doctors don't like to get involved in programs that don't pay anything.

"The migrants arrive on the job. They have no legal contract stating wages or length of work. The housing conditions are deplorable. Usually there are two or three possibilities. Some farmers build wooden houses. There are government guidelines, but in most cases those guidelines are ignored. And there are state camps, provided by various states, which are usually inadequate. Most do not have hot water. Nor adequate toilet facilities. I was living in one camp, for about three hundred people, and it had four toilets for the men and an equal number for the women. They were filthy." He pointed out that if the worker and his family do not get housing provided by the farmer or by the state he must try to find an abandoned rundown house and live in it.

The priest stayed in a South Carolina swampy farm area "and when the tides came in, the workers had to move their furniture and this was usually twice a day. They're stuck in the wooded areas and snakes get in the houses. And in the summer along the coast the mosquitoes are terrible.

"The migrants are not protected with any life insurance while they work. They do not get bonuses if they do a good job or if the farmer gets a good crop and a high yield. And they must keep going, in freezing rains or under a hot, blazing sun. Stooping, picking. I couldn't do it, probably not for two hours, especially in the heat of the day. The migrants get up about five in the morning and work until six or seven at night. They are probably the hardest working people in the United States."

After my visit with Father Dyer, I talk with Catholic sisters in Washington, D.C., who operate the East Coast Migrant Health Project. Through them, I arrange a visit with Peggy Weber, a registered nurse and director of a health center for farm workers near Middletown, New York. Peggy, who is of Indian heritage, recognizes Indian characteristics among the Mexican migrants. "You see it in their submissiveness, their passivity—you may describe it as 'acceptance.' Yet they are strong and endure hardships with little complaint, belligerency, or arrogance. I think you find arrogance more among the Puerto Ricans. But you don't find anger and hostility among the Mexicans. I think that's the difference. You don't find any anger."

It may be there, however. And it is my idea that it is. What is most hidden is most real.

Peggy Weber feels an empathy for the Mexicans. But she points out that in the community where she works "there's an animosity toward them, because they are 'different,' because they don't speak English. It's a tremendous barrier. I try to explain that they are poorest of all, the most neglected, that they die at an average age of 49. But the Anglos, the blacks, and the Puerto Ricans who live here don't understand, they resent the health clinic services to the migrants."

Peggy—in her 30s, six feet tall, dynamic, and attractive—has worked with the Mexican families for eight years, and speaks of them as she would of her own family. "There's something about the Mexicans that is different. First of all, I believe many of them enjoy working the land. There's nothing wrong with that, I just think you have to improve their working conditions. Most of them are like my grandfather—he was a farmer all of his life. People have to understand that Mexicans enjoy the land. They feel an identity with it, they cling to it, even though the land belongs to others who may underpay and overwork and abuse them.

"Someone has said that if we didn't have the Mexican farm workers, the legals and the illegals, we would not have food on our tables. There is some truth in that," Peggy continues. "Certainly in all parts of the United States a large part of the food we eat has been planted, nurtured, and harvested by Mexican field workers. They have a hand in our food industry from the field to the corner grocery store."

Peggy Weber also believes most people overlook what migrants contribute economically to a community. For example, Pine Island, just an hour and half north of New York City, has a population for six months of the year that is more than half Mexican. Each spring with the influx of migrant farm workers from Texas the town's population swells from five hundred to around a thousand. "They come in. They live here, shop here, for six months. They spend a lot of money. What they spend on food alone contributes enormously to this county," Peggy says.

The Mexicans and other migrants work for 50 Orange County growers who produce onions, potatoes, lettuce, and celery. One of the growers, Tony LaScala, hires only Mexican field workers. His foreman, Junior Rodriguez, a former migrant who "settled out" to work full time for LaScala now travels to the Rio Grande Valley each winter to recruit workers for the following spring. "It's a simple matter. The families tell me if they plan to come. If they give their word, you can count on them," Rodriguez relates. "We pay $2.50 an hour, plus LaScala gives each worker $35 on arrival, to defray their automobile expenses in getting here, and another $35 when they leave. LaScala also provides the housing and pays electricity, gas, and water for them."

Tony LaScala, dressed in work clothes, is supervising the unloading of onions for winter storage when I meet him. "You see, I get dirty and I work right along with the others," he says, with an obvious delight in his prowess. "I can do any type of job that needs to be done, planting, clipping onions, tending the fields, running a tractor and other large equipment."

His father came from Italy to this country in 1910, "settling on this rich, black soil where once there was a glacial lake. He cleared the land with a hoe and his back. Today the land is as productive as lower California, or, for that matter, as any in the world." A former pilot on a Navy carrier in the Pacific, LaScala came home from World War II to take his father's place as head of the farm. Now in his late 50s, of medium build, with reddish-brown hair, he likes to push his energies to the limit. It's the only way, he believes, you stay healthy.

However hard he might try to work, he says, "the Mexicans will outwork you." Also, they have other qualities: "the Mexicans work in family groups and are more stable than Puerto Ricans, blacks, or any other of the field workers. The families come together, stay together. They are loyal. . . . I have found out that if you earn the respect of the Mexican, he'll do anything for you."

Each year the same families travel north with the regularity of migrating birds. Mothers and daughters pack tortillas and tacos for the trip. Families of up to 12, including mother, father, children, aunts, uncles, and cousins crowd into ancient automobiles and station wagons. Fathers and sons take turns at the wheel. They drive straight through, from the Mexican border to New York State, a distance of more than two thousand miles, with only restroom and fuel stops. They report to LaScala each year by April 1. Most of them have documents LaScala accepts as "legal" although, as pointed out, the legality of documents is difficult to ascertain.

By late April the families are planting celery and onions. They're weeding celery in July. When the celery is ready to harvest they cut it up for celery hearts and clip onions. LaScala and I drive in an old sedan across fields of onions sprouting from the black dirt. We stop alongside a harvesting machine. "That's a father-son team. They've been with me for ten years. The father is 'Polo' Hernandez, he's operating the truck. And the machine is run by his son, Pepe." Pointing to Pepe's hand signals indicating Polo should accelerate or slow the truck, Lascala says, "They've the same perfect timing as a conductor and first violinist."

The machine cost $40,000, but regardless of high costs, growers are being forced into more and more mechanization "because no one but the Mexicans want to work." LaScala formerly hired five hundred workers. "Eventually I'll be working with only five or six large Mexican families."

Early the next morning, equipped with a pair of clippers like large scissors, I join the migrants. Guadalupe Gonzalez, a mother of eight, explains: "Use your left hand to pull up the onions, then, the clippers in your right hand, you cut the tops." I bend double, slowly moving along endless rows of onions, endlessly repeating what she has shown me. We leave the green tops in the fields and toss the onions into a box we drag beside us.

Guadalupe Gonzalez tells me she has a husband working in the field, as well as a daughter Lupeta, 19, who will return shortly to school in the Rio Grande Valley. Olga, 15, Hortensia, 14, and a younger son also are clipping onions. They do not want to return to school. Guadalupe Gonzalez is unhappy about this because she feels they will miss the opportunity to change their pattern of life and to rise out of the migrant stream. I see her as a serious, hard-working mother, and I am attracted to her because of her strength of character. Yet there is a sadness, a resignation about her, a bitterness that is hidden behind her gentleness and passivity.

I ask Guadalupe what she thinks about joining a union. "It brings too many problems," she replies. Perhaps she thinks she should say that. She knows that even with the César Chavez leadership in California, workers are often fired for union activities. No other state has a Chavez, and he has not branched out from California. She counts her few benefits: "Here if we want to work 60 hours a week, we can do so. This way I can earn $150 a week." That's considered very good for a farm worker. Also, Guadalupe and the others appreciate the free housing LaScala gives them, and his paying their expenses to and from Texas. But much of this smacks of the old *patrón* system, where the boss is "good" to his servants.

There are no toilet facilities in the field. Angela Hernandez, 19, whose father and brother work the harvesting machine, walks with me to the bushes. I motion to some I think offer us some privacy, but Angela is more modest. She shakes her head and indicates we should walk further. Modesty is ingrained among the farm workers. Women are very careful when undressing in front of other women. When taking a shower, if another woman is around, a woman will keep on her underclothes until she has a towel around her.

I stay with the migrants in their housing units, made of cinder blocks, with concrete floors, and bunk beds. Two or three families, or a total of about 25 people, share kitchen facilities and a toilet.

The camp that LaScala provides certainly is better than the "slave camps" that Father Dyer visited. And

LaScala is an unusual boss, admiring the Mexicans as he does and enjoying working alongside them. But LaScala could sell his farm tomorrow and the workers would have a different boss, perhaps one who held them as prisoners and worked them under armed guard. Few outsiders, except a few daring souls such as Father Dyer ever enter those camps.

From the LaScala farm, I travel to California, to work with field laborers in César Chavez' union. In Tijuana, across the border from San Diego, I lived successively with the families of Lola Barragan and Pascual Jiménez Martínez.

In the Jiménez Martínez home, an alarm sounds at 4:30 A.M. I dress hurriedly, pulling on old denim pants, a long-sleeved shirt, socks, tennis shoes. At 4:45 A.M., while the rest of the family is still sleeping, we walk outside in the darkness.

Pascual takes a pail of water, dashes it across the windshield of his 1963 Ford sedan to sluice away the dust. We begin our drive. In Pascual's barrio I see no pavement or sidewalks. There is no sanitation or sewage, no drainage ditches, no street lights, parks, grassy lawns, or shade trees. His headlights search out the barren nothingness of the brown Tijuana hills. Soon, heading toward the Port of Entry, I see the headlights of other cars. Pascual is like tens of thousands of laborers who wake in Mexico and commute to work in the United States.

As Pascual and I drive in the predawn from Mexico toward the United States, he talks to me about the millions of Mexican workers who have traveled north from Mexico to work in the fields of the Anglos.

His father was one of the workers recruited in Mexico under the bracero program. Pascual says he believes the Mexican government was at first reluctant to allow United States Labor Department officials to come into their country and recruit their people, as if they were

commodities for rent to a stronger power. "But, Mexico
eventually agreed." Before then, entries into the United
States from Mexico had been mostly "migration by
drift." But in World War II the migration was initiated,
supervised, and regulated by the United States government. The Labor Department sent its representatives to
set up large recruitment centers.

"My father was recruited in Hermosillo, in Baja California." Other large centers were in Mexico City,
Chihuahua, and Monterrey. The United States flag and
the flag of Mexico were flown in all the recruitment
camps. Once the senior Jiménez had signed on as a
bracero he was handed a small laminated card that
permitted him to cross into the United States.

Dawn breaks as Pascual continues to talk to me about
his father. I study Pascual's features. He looks very
Indian, with high cheekbones and straight, black, shoulder-length hair.

Pascual makes a turn and we are on pavement, heading
into a different world through the Port of Entry. It's the
busiest port in the world—one hundred twenty thousand
persons come and go here every day, most by automobile,
some walking. Although 16 lanes lead out of Tijuana, the
traffic is bumper to bumper as early as 5:00 A.M.

"It's interesting," Pascual relates, as we sit waiting,
"my father was sent first to California's Imperial Valley,
just where we are heading." Jiménez was one of fifty-
three thousand Mexican workers recruited in 1942. In
1944 we recruited more than sixty-two thousand. In 1945
we increased recruitment to one hundred twenty thousand workers. In those years, Mexicans composed about
80 percent of the field laborers in southern California and
they still do.

"My father was recruited for six months' to a year's
work at a time," Pascual continues. Like other braceros,
he was contracted for seasonal work and when the job

was finished he was sent back to Mexico. "The growers could get braceros on a 48-hour notice—as many as they might need and for as long or as short a period as they wanted them. They did not have to guarantee them anything. If any one of them talked about working less than 10 or 12 hours or getting more money the grower could call law-enforcement officers who would expel him for bad behavior. There were millions more where he came from."

Pascual's father, even in his day, had spoken out for better working conditions, and Pascual did too. When I first met him, he had been fired from the Robert Richardson ranch for union activities. Having no field work he became a volunteer in César Chavez' Farm Workers Union. "I was paid $5 a week. It's been increased now to $10 a week. Plus you get expenses including the essential food for your family." After nine months of struggle, the field workers won bargaining rights. Richardson was forced to rehire the workers and give them back pay.

Our car inches up to a border guard at the Port of Entry. We show our passports and continue toward the Imperial Valley near San Diego. Pascual parks his car near a vast field of tomatoes. Other cars and station wagons, all of ancient vintage, pull up and workers greet each other. Most of these workers, Pascual believes, have working papers. All up and down the coast, however, growers hire tens of thousands of illegals. A few illegal farm workers carry out-dated, worthless bracero cards. Other illegal farm workers carry Social Security cards. "The union today," Pascual says, "signs on anyone who wants to work. We don't ask if you are legal or not."

One couple, Seferino and his wife Tona, who both work in the fields, cook tortillas on a flat sheet of iron placed over a fire log. Selling the tortillas brings them a few extra pennies. I share a quick breakfast with several workers: tacos and tortillas with hot, sweetened coffee from a thermos jug.

At 7:00 A.M., a whistle blows. Each of us slips on gloves and a hat for protection from the sun. Each takes a wooden box or *caja* and enters one of the rows of tomatoes that, as far as I can discern, stretch north to infinity. As if I were climbing a mountain, I do not consider what may be insurmountable, but take a step at a time. I keep pace with Pascual in the next row. There's a rhythm: you bend, swiftly pluck a tomato from the plants and toss it into the box. You keep moving. You push or drag the *caja* as you go. Because I am a visitor, helping Pascual, I am not being paid. He and the other pickers—there are 84 men and women in this field—are earning the new wage scale, $3 an hour.

The grower, Robert Richardson, a large, serious, hard-driving man, comes to the fields. He seems suspicious of my motives. He may be wondering if I am a representative of the union, perhaps a rabble-rouser or Communist, sent out from Washington.

I can understand what he feels. I grew up in Texas when most people linked union organizers with rabble-rousers and Communists. I felt what the majority felt: that unions were bad—and must be kept out.

Pascual, educated in the United States, completely bilingual and thoroughly familiar with the history of our unions, explains that in every state except California farm workers are excluded from the right to union elections.

"If you look at labor laws, in practically every area, the farm workers are excluded," Pascual says. "Congress did away with children working in the sweatshops and factories. I think the law was passed in 1935. However farm workers were excluded from that. That was 42 years ago, and except for a few of us here in California, farm workers are still excluded."

After the long battle over the union contract, tension and suspicion is a part of the air we breathe. The Mexicans around me, however, see their boss as a misguided soul and they do not show whatever bitterness they may feel toward him. Among themselves, the workers call him "Bobby," indicating that they recognize no social distance between themselves and the land-owner.

Learning to pick tomatoes takes about five minutes. Then, for me, the job becomes repetitive, tedious, weari-some. Working hard makes the time go faster. Still, an hour passes like a week. I fill my box with tomatoes. Then, dropping my work gloves beside the plant I've last plucked, I lug the *caja* to a loading truck. Here, I get an empty wooden box, walk back along the endless row of tomatoes until I find the gloves, pull them on, bend over double, and in this ape-like position, I pluck, move, pluck.

At 10:00 A.M., a foreman blows a whistle. Pascual and I are near the end of a row and I move over to his row. Both of us, welcoming this break, collapse to a sitting position in the dirt. I have pushed myself hard for three hours. For the past 30 minutes, I tell Pascual I was moved more by willpower than physical strength. And, I add, I don't think I could have continued without this break.

"Until March, 1977, there was not one single company that was giving the ten-minute break," Pascual tells me. "Yet, it is a state law. We filed complaints all over the place. We had no toilets or else dirty toilets. No drinking water. No wash water. Some workers had to live in caves, under trees, anywhere. In some migrant camps, they slept in barracks, 20 to 30 stuffed in a room. Some were furnished blankets, some were not. If they had tortillas and beans, that was a lot. One day armed men in eight patrol cars—and with dogs—converged on us. Growers have the power to use the police to intimidate us. Workers were picking crops from 7:00 A.M. to 9:00 P.M.,

with no guarantee of wages, no medical plan, no griev-
ance procedures against firings for union organizing. We
were treated like animals and we would be loaded on flat-
bed trucks with no guard rails and hauled to various fields
at incredible speeds. Several workers fell and broke their
legs and arms. Foremen abused and shouted at the
workers: 'Animals, let's go!' Now, with the union, people
are less afraid to protest."

A whistle sounds and we resume work. Then I overhear
shouts of profanity. "You son-of-a-bitch," the foreman
yells to Alfred "Minnie" López. "If you don't want to
work, get back to Mexico!" A diminutive man, "Minnie"
López maintains he is working and returns the son-of-a-
bitch barrage adding the foreman can go to hell. Immediately Minnie is surrounded by his union friends. "If you
want to make an issue of this," Pascual tells the foreman,
"you can get two witnesses, we'll get two witnesses and
we'll have a hearing."

"No, no," the foreman backs off. He tells everyone to
get back to the job.

We all resume work. "Without the union 'Minnie'
would have been fired instantly," Pascual tells me.
Taking insults has always been the hardest part of field
work. A worker usually is so beaten down by insults he
can't stand up for his rights. But we've gained a few
privileges now and they mean so much: a jug from which
you can get a cup of water, having the use of a clean
toilet. Before the foreman would say: 'You Mexicans will
get sick at your stomach if you drink water on this side.'
Once we said we'd like to pool some money and get some
ice. It was our money. But he said, 'Oh no, you will get
sick in the head if you have ice.' "

Workers at the end of the day like to change into clean
clothes. "We had the use of an old shed, but one day
Bobby locked it, saying 'I need it for storage,'" Pascual
relates. "We took it up with the union, and the union

ruled a grower could not remove rights or privileges we previously had enjoyed, and Bobby had to unlock the shed."

It's surprising how quickly Pascual and I fill boxes with tomatoes. On a good day, when the vines are heavy, Pascual can fill 100 boxes. Each *caja* is called a field box. And each field box makes two boxes at the packing shed.

I notice the plants all have a heavy whitish cast of leaves due to poisonous sprays. As the nation's number one agricultural state, California accounts for about 20 percent of the pesticides used throughout the nation every year. Ranging from relatively innocuous to extremely toxic, the chemicals do everything from killing weeds in cotton or tiny bugs in orchards to preventing mold on peaches or turning cannery tomatoes red in a hurry.

Growers such as Richardson use pesticides and herbicides to ward off weeds as well as heavy insect infestation such as nematodes. They say they need to use fungicides to prevent soil diseases called verticillium and fusarium that wilt and kill tomato plants. "Workers are constantly exposed to the pesticides and herbicides," Pascual says. He recalls a poisoning incident in the Madera Vineyards near Fresno. The vineyards were illegally sprayed with heavy applications of Torak, an organophosphate pesticide that can affect the central nervous system, causing blurred vision, nausea, headaches, and muscle tremors. "Workers, not knowing of the poisonous sprays, went into the vineyards, and began to crumble with pain. One hundred twenty workers became violently ill. Eighty required medical treatment.

"I got sick once," Pascual continues. "We were working in a field that had just been sprayed. I got a stuffy head and nose. It wasn't a cold. But I couldn't breathe. I went to a doctor and he said it was the spray on the tomatoes. They were using DDT and a chemical for the weeds both

at the same time." Dr. Joseph Swartz, an Environmental
Protection Agency biophysicist-researcher, has called
farm work "one of the most hazardous occupations," not
because the work itself will break your back or kill you,
but because poisonous sprays can damage or ruin your
health.

At 12 noon, a whistle blows. It's time for a 30-minute
lunch break. We pile aboard two trucks that deliver us to
the parking area. Most workers sit beside their vehicles,
on the ground, eating home-cooked lunches of corn
tortillas with small chunks of chilies and ground meat.
Others pile in a car and speed to a nearby carry-out
restaurant for chips, burgers, and colas.

After lunch, we again are back in the rows. One worker
starts to sing. Another joins and then a third. Others
listen to small radios they carry around their waists.
Always there is joking. They have a spirit, a goal, a unity,
and a caring, one for the other. I have not known such a
feeling since the religious revival meetings I attended as
a child. Their striving for a better life is infectious.
Despite burdens that have destroyed millions of others,
the survivors exude confidence and even a sense of joy.

Many Anglos would not understand a man like Pascual
remaining in the arduous, dirty field work when as a
United States citizen he could "better" himself, move on
up an economic ladder. Pascual, however, has an Indian
heritage, and the Indian has a value system different
than that of the Anglo. He does not put the dollar first.
Being is more important than achieving. Pascual,
however, has tried other jobs. For instance, once he
worked in an electronic plant and made more than double
what he makes in the fields, but he did not like being in a
windowless plant all day.

He likes farm work: "I like sowing the seeds, setting
out small plants. Building stakes and tying the plants to
them for protection. And trimming the plants when they
grow tall. I like being near the earth. When it's hot. Or

when it's cold. Even in the rain. I like the smell of the air, of the plants. I like to see the sky. I am not happy staying inside a building all day. All of nature is shut out. I feel I lose my time. So I am happy when I come to the fields. This work is too hard. But *gracias a Dios* I am able to do it."

Hearing Pascual identify himself with the soil, I momentarily relive my childhood days on the wide open plains of West Texas. My father taught me to plant tomato seeds and to nurture the small plants. When dark clouds threatened storms with rain and hail, I would run to protectively place a quart fruit jar over each fledgling plant. As the plants matured, we tied them to stakes, as Pascual described. Growing up, I remember the smell of the plants. They were pungent, fresh, fruity. The plants produced luscious, red vine-ripened tomatoes. I would sometimes bite into one, as I would an apple. It was like tasting sunshine.

I compare those home-grown tomatoes of my childhood with the hard, bright green ones I am picking. They feel like baseballs. "You can drop one from a second-story window and its contents won't burst its chemically-protected skin," Pascual says.

As I move along, I constantly step on the best of the products, the fully matured, alive, red, juicy tomatoes that are left to rot. Can't someone pick them up? I ask Pascual. Can't they be given to hungry people?

"No," he replies. "It's good food, but we can't pick them up. Bobby gets mad when you take five or six of the ones that will go to waste."

Every farm worker, Pascual says, has watched vast fields go to rot if the grower does not get the price he wants. "One grower who signed a contract with us in 1975 let a field of tomatoes rot so he could bill insurance and not give the workers anything. The grower can get a subsidy from the government and then more money from insurance."

To Pascual it does not make sense that the United States government pours so much money into helping big growers. "It would be different in Mexico. Mexico should help the farmer. Almost half of the Mexican population tries to make a living on very small farms. Farming is still very much of a family business. But not in this country. It's a huge industry, like the steel or automobile industries. Agriculture is about the biggest industry here in California—and in the United States, for that matter. Growers don't need the government giving them handouts."

As an example of the money in agriculture, Pascual says, "Yesterday I picked 47 *cajas*, or field boxes, of tomatoes. That's $1,000 worth of tomatoes. Yesterday 87 workers picked over $40,000 worth of tomatoes."

Overhead I hear the constant buzzing of aircraft. And I see an Armed Forces helicopter. I know former President Nixon lives just up the beach at San Clemente. The Cessna in which I had ridden with a Border Patrol pilot drones past searching for wets. If the pilot were to ask other agents to raid this field, all of us working here would need to prove citizenship—or go to jail.

As a people we have mixed emotions about Mexican farm workers, both the legals and the illegals. They have been extremely good for our economy. As Pascual pointed out, agriculture and the agribusiness is the number one industry in this country. The profits would not be there without the cheap farm labor.

We *want* the cheap labor. And yet we dislike seeing pictures of hungry, cold workers in our fields, whose children cannot go to school because they must work alongside their parents to earn enough to survive.

To get cheap labor, some people believe we must keep the Mexicans scared—with frequent raids that frighten both the illegals and the legals.

As an indication of our ambivalence toward illegals,

Immigration Commissioner Castillo told me: "I guess one very famous Chicano leader sort of summed it up very well. He said: 'I don't want to send them back because they are coming over just as my family did, but on the other hand I don't want them here because they might take jobs away from my union.' So he's in a dilemma."

Meanwhile, so are the illegals and the legals. In truth, we are all in the dilemma together.

ELEVEN

This Promised Land

Several of those who have studied Mexican immigration over a number of years have concluded that the majority of illegals do not come here hoping to get United States citizenship. Rather it has been deduced that they prefer to retain their Mexican citizenship and come here only when necessary to earn enough to support their families back home.

I listened to many Mexican men in our prisons who confirmed this. I recall especially one young illegal who had been clearing tables in a restaurant. Customers had called him a Mexican American, a Chicano, and he told me: "I was embarrassed." He added, proudly: "I am Mexican."

But I heard an entirely different story from the Mexican women I interviewed in our jails. They, indeed, saw this as a Promised Land to which they wanted to come permanently, cutting their ties to a past that linked them in servitude to a man: a father, or a husband or a lover. To many of these women, getting papers to work in the United States means they no longer need to be poor. And, equally important to many, not being poor means no longer needing to be dominated by a man.

Valera Cazares, 18, in a Brooklyn jail for entering the country illegally, told me she has seen her mother dominated by her father, who always kept her pregnant, and that her oldest sister, a mother of five, has been abandoned by her husband. Valera, an attractive, slender woman, with shoulder-length, black hair, is determined she will have a different life.

"I came to get a job because in Mexico it's very hard to find work unless you have a good education. Here there's always work. I came here to struggle," she said, her dark eyes intense with purpose. She does not smoke, drink hard liquor, or have a boy friend. Besides her mother and father, she has five sisters and two brothers.

In Mexico, she explained, only a lucky few go to school. "It costs too much." But one of the lucky ones, she enrolled in a business school and had completed a year and a half of shorthand, typing, translating, commerce, banking, and bookkeeping. "I only needed five months to finish, I had thought I would have an opportunity to go to school here."

I suggest the traditional: She might "fall in love" and get married. No, she said, "definitely not. I want a job to support myself and to help my family. That is my goal." I suggest a Mexican woman must have courage to leave her family and country and come to a land where she has no relatives and no job. "It's not courage I lack," she says. "It's only a little money."

Such a woman, with her desire to control her own life, will not be easily deterred. She was soon to be deported to Mexico. But I feel certain that Valera Cazares somehow will finish her business course and find a job, either in Mexico or in the States, that will enable her to pay her own rent and buy her own food. And live with some small idea that she is guardian of her life. She will risk her life to win what most Anglo woman take for granted.

I always identified especially with the women prisoners. I crossed three times without papers and without being caught, but I always imagined—seeing a woman prisoner—that I was standing in her shoes. Once in Border Patrol headquarters near San Diego an agent came in with a young woman. Another agent, W. D. Burt, seeing her, told the arresting officer he had apprehended the same woman a week earlier. "I remember her face. I talked with her a long time because there was a *coyote* involved." Then, he recalled, "She first claimed to be a United States citizen." She is 17, with long, straight hair to her waist and a childlike expression. She has 250 pesos, about $10. "I came over to buy a cake," she tells the officers. They do not believe her.

She is standing alongside another woman. Neither apparently knows the other. The teen-ager looks innocent; the other, with short hair dyed red and in her mid-thirties, impresses me as a woman who must believe she is 65. Both are standing as before a bar of justice—a counter that separates them from the officer who interrogates them. I stand alongside the women.

The officer, questioning the red-haired woman demands: "Where were you going?"

"Anywhere," she replies, in a desperate tone. Both women, nice looking, neatly dressed, are brushing back tears. They are not criminals, they are guilty as I am guilty, guilty of wanting to better myself, to be in a position to realize my best potential.

I go with Burt to put the woman in the "cage" compartment of his van. He will drive them to the border. Momentarily I wonder: where will I sit? I feel like a hypocrite, knowing that I belong to their sisterhood, yet separating myself, aligning myself with the oppressor, Up Front.

Luck has placed us in these positions. I now have the

law on my side, I am legal. Also, it is a cold night. And I
have a coat. I turn from my Up Front position and ask
through the wire that separates us: Aren't you cold?

"Yes," one says softly.

Burt starts the motor and we are off, his radio blaring
the voice of a dispatcher. I quietly say to Burt: Neither of
the two women has a coat. They must be cold.

"They left Mexico in the daytime, when it was warm,"
he reminds me. "It would have been suspect if they had
carried any coat. Besides," he adds, "they might not have
one."

Burt does not believe the red-haired woman is from
Mexico. "They say they are so they will only be deported
as far as the border, then they can cross over again." Like
most Anglos who speak some Spanish, he does not know
the language well enough to distinguish a Mexican from
a Peruvian, a Colombian, or any of the other Spanish-
speaking peoples.

We drive to the Port of Entry. He unlocks a gate in the
fence. "Wait here," he says and leaves us.

I am holding the gate. They could run—but where?

He returns with a Mexican Customs official who leads
them away. I am left to ponder their future. I know they
have dreamed a dream, and they believe they can best
realize it in the United States.

In striving for this dream, the Mexican illegal has been
enormously influenced by the mass media of the United
States. Scores of Mexico City theaters show Hollywood
films. One hundred and three American television programs are regularly shown in Mexico City via Cablevi-
sion. Also, American radio and television broadcasting go
direct to Mexicans living in the borderlands. The potential audience for this programming is three or four
million people.

I asked the illegal women I interviewed in our jails:
How did you learn about life in the United States?

Many said they saw United States movies and television shows or heard United States radio programs. Also, many said they occasionally saw such publications as *Reader's Digest, Time,* or *Good Housekeeping* in Spanish.

Moreover, with seven of our largest Madison Avenue advertising agencies operating in Mexico City, we constantly sell the Mexicans of the U.S.A. brand of the Good Way of Life. Our salesmanship encourages them to come here—legally and illegally. In interviewing both men and women illegals, I deduced that as long as only Mexican male illegals were crossing our border, the structure of the Mexican family back in Mexico remained intact. But now with women crossing to establish their independence in this Promised Land, the family back home will be entirely different.

Also, once the illegal Mexican woman gets here, she will have a far greater distance to travel on her road to liberation than either white or black women. Black women, who were kept out of white schools, had their own higher education institutions. The Hispanas have had none. They were never encouraged to leave home, to struggle for an education, to fend for themselves.

"The needs of Hispanas are different from needs of the majority of women in this country," believes Elisa Sánchez, president of an advocacy Chicana group called the Mexican American Women's National Association. Pointing out that over 75 percent of Mexican women in this country have a yearly income of below $5,000, Sánchez says the issue facing these women is survival. "Their needs consist of food, clothing, education, and health care."

The majority of Hispanas do not finish high school and thus do not acquire sufficient skill to allow them to enter a competitive labor market. "The majority will find only inadequately paid menial factory jobs or domestic jobs."

Available data, Sánchez continues, does not indicate that more Hispanas are graduating from professional schools, or entering managerial positions or becoming entrepreneurs. Rather, they are caught in an age-old trap: They continue to have large unplanned families, with not enough money to make it from day to day. They live in unsanitary and dilapidated housing that breeds all types of disease. They continue to show a greater incidence of uterince cancer and tuberculosis.

Sánchez, one of the 149 Hispanic women attending the National Women's Conference in 1977 in Houston, points out that Hispanas are a group tied most strongly to an ethnic and traditional culture. "Poverty and the lack of participation in the greater society has reinforced an inferior self-image among low-income Hispanas." But, she adds, this condition is being broken little by little.

I saw examples of this near our border when I interviewed two young women—one in Mexico and one in the United States—who a few years ago probably never would have dreamed of entering the work force. My meeting with the young women was arranged by a friend, Teresa Tijerina of McAllen, who happened to know both of them.

As we drove to pick them up, Teresa explained she has over the years watched the mushrooming of United States factories along the border.

First, Teresa and I meet Carmelina Rodriguez. Then crossing the border into Mexico we pick up Celia Hernandez and the four of us drive to the San Carlos cafe, across from the Central Plaza in Reynosa.

Walking into the cafe, I am aware that a few years ago it would be scandalous for four unescorted women to enter a Mexican cafe late at night. I am interested in the economic changes that have made such social changes possible. Over cold drinks, the young women explain they are part of the work force hired by the 700 United States companies who have moved to the Mexican border.

The United States firms, they say, like to hire young

Mexican women. Eighty-five percent of their employees are women from 16 to 22 years of age, and most of them are unmarried.

Carmelina is 23 and lives in McAllen. "My mother was born in Mexico, but my father was born in Texas, and because he was a United States citizen, I could claim his citizenship." She is tall, attractive, self-assured.

Her first job in an office on the United States side of the border was for International Fruit Shippers and Growers. The company, she explains, buys melons, oranges, pineapples, and mangoes in Mexico and sells them in the United States.

She currently works for the Meredian Manufacturing Company in Hidalgo, Texas, that makes jackets for men and women. "We cut the material in the United States, then send it to Mexico for sewing. They send the jackets back and we ship them out to stores throughout the United States. The jackets are all labeled 'Made in U.S.A.'"

She earns $2.60 an hour. "I work eight hours a day, with an hour off for lunch. For a 40-hour week, I make $104. I get a one-week's paid vacation. This year I'm going to Acapulco. My dream? I know what I do *not* want. I do *not* want to get married. Rather, my ambition is to travel, to see all the world."

The other factory worker, Celia Hernández, who is 17 and a Mexican citizen, listens, fascinated to hear a young woman say she does not want to get married. Celia began life in a way that is all too traditional for dirt-poor Mexicans. "I got married at 14. And when I was six-months pregnant my husband left me." She never considered an abortion. She was not yet 15 when she gave birth to a son.

She lives with her mother, a woman who is unmarried, has nine children, and who sews to make a living. Celia's youngest brother is three. One brother, 13, works as a pharmacy delivery boy, and another, 16, works as a mechanic.

Celia impresses me as what writers once called a typical feminine creature. She is quiet, vulnerable, shy, humble, a woman, her sad eyes indicate, who will always forgive. Seeing her, I think of the adage about the violet forgiving the heel that crushes it.

"I always dreamed of being a dancer, a ballerina," she relates. "I hear music, and I sense a movement in my body that is mystical, *siento algo raro.* I know I have this ability, it was given to me by God. When I was 13 I won first prize in a dance contest. But we had no money for studies." Her dark eyes express the hopelessness of her dream. I note her fragile body, her beauty, her long glistening black hair tied back with a ribbon. Also I note front teeth beginning to decay.

Celia, showing us the palms of her hands, with callouses, relates that she works for KIMCO, a manufacturer of parts for electric organs. "The steel material for the organs comes from Indiana to McAllen, and from there it's sent to Reynosa, and we turn it into cables and then ship them back to Indiana."

Mondays through Fridays, Celia gets up at five, packs her lunch, leaves the house at six, takes a 15-cent, hour-long bus ride and punches in at 7:30 A.M. and works until 5:36 P.M.

Five-thirty-*six?* I repeat.

"Yes, they want those extra minutes. If we didn't work until 5:36, they want us to work on Saturdays. It's supposed to be a nine-hour day. I earn 109 pesos a day, or about $5. It comes to $25 for a 45-hour week."

The workers, all young women, make the same salary. "We are never permitted to use a telephone or visit each other. At 10:00 A.M., a bell rings and we take a 10-minute break. I hurriedly stuff down some food. We get a 30-

minute break at lunch. At 3:00 P.M., I rush to get to a toilet. You can't relax for a moment."

Most of the plants, Celia says, hire young women "because we desperately need the money and because we are dependable."

Celia is dependable in that she does not miss work because of illness and is never late. But, like thousands of other young Mexican women, she has become a union member who marches and shouts for change.

Anglo employers who knew about liberated women in New York, Boston, Chicago, and Los Angeles clearly did not expect to see their sisters emerge so soon in Reynosa, Juárez, and Tijuana. They recruited women because they were "docile" and not organized in unions. But employers no longer can be sure of Mexican women. They have been quick to organize and articulate their demands.

It is significant that the first International Womens Year Conference was held in 1976 in Mexico City. Perhaps nowhere else in the world are women's lives changing more rapidly. Even so, the quest for equality in Mexico remains light years behind the liberation of women in the United States. Most Mexicans could still serve as perfect examples of unliberated women: They are submissive creatures living in the shadow of domineering men.

In McAllen, I met a woman like this. María Juliana Alvarez de Espinosa, born in 1904 in Guanajuato, was 14 when she married Tertuliano Alvarez, who was 54. "He was jealous, he beat me," she relates, showing me marks alongside her right eye made 60 years ago.

Her husband took cattle to market in Mexico City, and got paid in gold. "He came back and buried the gold under the house. When he died, I had no sense of money. And even after he was dead, he somehow continued to dominate me, I felt he was still around. I remained frightened of him. I was afraid to take *his* money from

its hiding place. I was certain if I did, he would come back
and beat me.

"My elder daughter Ninfa, then about 15, sold the
house on a whim for the equivalent of $25 because she
wanted to buy a new dress. I did not contest her verbal
sale. I was a totally ignorant, submissive creature. People
took possession of the house, moving me out. With the
house they got the gold buried under it, and also a
collection of valuable pistols and household items. Now I
wonder how anyone could have been so naïve, so ignorant, but I had been kept a virtual slave to my husband. I
could not think or move on my own initiative."

Some years later she married another man, a bracero
worker in the United States, who never beat her and who
taught her how to manage money.

In my travels in Mexico I saw how much the appearance of women has changed in thirty years. In the
1940s a woman stayed behind doors that opened for her
only to shop or to go to mass. She impressed me generally
as a woman who was faithful, unthinking, subservient,
and inferior. She served the man. Sacrificed for him. She
obeyed her father and bowed to the wishes of her
brothers, her husband, her sons. Three decades ago I
often rode by horseback in rural Mexico or went by jeep
over rough mountain terrain, and for such journeys I
wore a shirt and trousers. In remote villages with no
electricity or telephones and little contact with the
outside world, I would walk alone in a central plaza,
aware that the eyes of curious women peered at me from
behind drawn shades. I met many such women when
their husbands invited me into their homes, and the
sheltered wives told me they had never met a woman who
dressed like a man.

For a while I lived on an isolated ranch on the vast
mauve plains of central Chihuahua. The owners were in
Europe and I was the only person residing in the large,

rambling house. Each day I sat outside typing in a sun-filled patio. The wives of the cowboys who lived in small adobe *casas* back of the big house would gather around me, and repeat incredulously: Where was the man in my life? The man who told me what to do? Did I live alone? *Sola?* They gasped in amazement at the idea. They said they had never met a woman who lived her life as she—and not a man—determined life should be lived.

One of the women had 19 children. I asked if she planned to have another. Then I realized that this woman could not imagine that she might control such events in her life. Eventually she said:

"I do not believe Dios will bless me with another child."

I mentally have compared that woman in her tradi-tional role with the illegal women I interviewed in our jails who are struggling for a different lifestyle.

The illegal Mexican women are moving rapidly into the twentieth century. How they dress indicates how much they have moved in their thinking. In 1977 most of the documented and undocumented women I interviewed wore slacks and shirts. Their attire spoke as eloquently as their words: They were leaving protective walls and protective men. Today undocumented women are cross-ing a frontier, being chased by the police, risking their lives. They swim a river. Race across freeways. They work in cotton fields, pick tomatoes, clip onions, work in factories.

"The single most important development of the twen-tieth century," the financial writer Sylvia Porter has observed, "is the pouring of women into the labor force."

Traditionally, women around the world have seen their role to produce children, to be "blessed" by this oppor-tunity. They fit the description the American lexicogra-pher Noah Webster gives us for female: "designating or of the sex that produces ... offspring." Millions of Mexican women cling unthinkingly to the Roman Cath-olic teaching that it is a woman's duty to propagate the

earth—even if one does not have food for those you bring
into the world. This belief underlies the economic crisis in
Mexico, where the population explosion is the greatest in
the world.

One Mexican woman here illegally to earn money to
support six children told me she now uses the pill to
prevent more pregnancies. Another woman, a citizen, said
she is active in a campaign to lift the federal ban on
Medicaid-funded abortions. "If a woman is receiving
Medicaid benefits, she is not able financially to pay for a
legal abortion," she relates. "She therefore has two choices:
She is forced to procreate, whether she wants to or not, or
she must seek an illegal abortion if she feels she has to end
her pregnancy." She added that "In Mexico, women only
now are beginning to realize that part of their independence is being able to afford not to have babies."

This, of course, means changes not only in the lives of
women, but in the structure of the families. Teresa
Tijerina, with whom I stayed in McAllen, had told me
that "the strength of the family" was the aspect that
distinguishes the Hispanic from the Anglo.

Hispanic women have in the past been long-suffering,
Teresa said. If they were not happy in their marriage
they never told it—until many years later. I witnessed
one such example. A group of us had driven to Mexico to
visit Teresa's Aunt Delia. After lunch the men disap-
peared outdoors. The women clustered on the porch.

What, I asked Aunt Delia, had her life been like—as a
woman? I studied her face, with her long hair pulled back
in a bun. Has she ever been to a beauty shop?

"Yes," she laughed, "once, for a wedding."

And does she ever use cosmetics?

"Only soap and water."

And what about jewelry?

"Only earrings."

And her husband, he died—nine years ago? She's
wearing black. Is she still in mourning?

"I wore black for seven years. Now I sometimes wear a dress that is both black and white."

Should she have died before her husband, would he have indicated by his clothing for seven years that he had lost a wife?

"Not necessarily. Sometimes a man will wear a black band for a brief time on his arm."

Has she ever wished she were born a man?

"Yes," she replied firmly. "I have often wished that. I would have had more freedom."

Teresa later told me she had never heard her Aunt Delia talk so frankly. But then, we reasoned, speaking frankly, after all these years, perhaps is part of her liberation.

Millions of women, who opt for the traditional woman's role, are not as lucky as Teresa. For instance, I once spent the night with the family of an illegal field laborer who works in San Diego. We were 13 people sleeping in a one-room slum shanty. There was little in the house except children, ages two months to 15 years. As the husband and I were leaving in a predawn hour to drive out into a world the wife can never see or know, a world of free movement, of interchange of adult conversations, ideas and laughter, I listened to her pathetic voice asking if he would be home that night. He goes and comes when he pleases. And yet not once in their married life has she gone out with friends. Probably, even if he now offered to stay home with the children, she would be like the woman whose husband buried gold under the house: She could not act with any initiative.

By doing farm labor, Mexican women—those here legally and illegally—are gaining more independence and taking a new look at the double standards that have existed for men and women. But while earning the freedom to work as men they still have the responsibilities, in most instances, of a wife and mother. Women working alongside men are not merely equal but are working harder because of their obligation to follow traditional patterns governing relationships between husband and wife. Psychologically this engenders a spirit of superiority in women and causes them to examine more closely the "double standard" that works to keep them subjugated.

In New York State, as I clipped onions alongside Guadalupe Gonzalez she commented, "This is only half my work. The other half is at home." She does all the housecleaning, all the shopping, all the washing of clothes, all the cooking. And although she works the same hours in the field as her husband José, he does not help with any household chores in the evenings.

While she is cooking, "he's busy being 'man,' *hombre*, taking it easy. He never helps. That would be beneath him." I suggested that young married couples would be different, that if both worked all day in the fields they would share the household work. "No," Guadalupe predicted, "It won't happen."

That evening in the migrant camp, near Middletown, New Jersey, I saw the newly-wed Petra Bejaran standing over a stove. In her 20s, she is six-months pregnant. Like Guadalupe and the other wives, she had worked the same hours as her husband. But in the camp, he rested, chatted with the men, drank a beer, while she worked two hours making tortillas and chili.

I visited Ernestina Gómez, a mother of six. The youngest, Jorge, one and a half years, stays in a day-care center while she clips onions. Did her husband help her with the chores? "No," she said, "He rests while I prepare supper. I get up at 4:00 A.M. and make five dozen tortillas for our breakfast and our lunch. And he sleeps as late as possible."

I detected great bitterness in the voices of these women who are trapped midstream in the liberation movement. Their husbands too are caught in a trap. They cannot make enough to provide for their families so their

wives must do field labor; but the men have been
indoctrinated over the centuries that it is unmanly to
assume a woman's role and feel they should not help with
the household chores.

One day I clipped onions alongside Angela Hernández,
19, petite, with shoulder-length hair and dimples. What
was her goal, her ambition, her greatest desire?

She raises her head from the black dirt and onions—a
far-away, wistful look in her eyes—and says in a fervent,
low voice: "To work in an office." She confided her dream
as another woman might say "to marry a millionaire,"
"to circle the globe," or "to become president." I reassure
her that she is young, intelligent. Getting work in an
office should be easy.

"It's not all that easy. This is the only thing I've ever
known. I've been working in the fields since I was 12. And
when you leave the family and this group, you are afraid
you are going to make a mistake, that someone will yell
at you. That's why we stay together. That's why we feel
secure among our own people. We don't feel secure
outside this circle. We don't know what to expect from
others. I know that when I am among the Anglos, I will
feel pains of insecurity and of inadequacies."

I mentioned she might meet someone and "fall in love."
Her jaws tighten. "If I do that, I won't ever get out of
this life. And my mother and all the older women know
that I should get out. Don't you hear the older women all
telling the younger ones, 'Go ahead and get your education. Don't let anyone or anything interfere.' They know
that there's another way. It is too late for them, but not
too late for me."

The Mexican women, here illegally and those here
legally, such as Angela, have much in common. They are
struggling to gain control over their lives. They believe
they have greater opportunities here than in Mexico. For
them, this is indeed a Promised Land.

Where Do We Go from Here?

All through this book I have drawn an analogy between the war on our doorstep and the no-win war we fought in Vietnam.

Vietnam is important to us all. And specifically to me because, as a reporter, I saw that hospitals there were filled with women and children we had bombed. How, I wondered, can we do this to a people? And I knew: We can do it because we do not *see* them. We make them invisible.

In pre-Civil Rights days when we refused to "see" a black as equal to a white, Ralph Ellison wrote his classic, *The Invisible Man*. He, a black, was telling the rest of us: You look right through me. You don't see me. The blacks then forced us to change. And we gained a new vision that enabled us to "see" blacks.

We Anglos still are myopic, however, when it comes to

those who are brown. Not many years ago, a historian, George Sánchez, referred to the Spanish-speaking as "an orphan group, the least known, the least sponsored and the least vocal large minority in the nation." As recently as 1966 a spokesman for those of Spanish descent said, "We're the best kept secret in America."

Among aggressive, materialistic whites and blacks, who have very similar values, the brown Mexicans are too easily lost. Their characteristic gentleness, their love of nature and the earth, make them different from most of us. We do not tolerate too much difference in people. This, I believe, is why we wage a war against them but are indifferent toward the white illegals who come into this country.

John F. Kennedy once said, "We are a nation of immigrants." But each wave of newcomers has had to fight for its place here. The Immigration Service—that now throws most of its manpower and dollars into a war against Mexican illegals—was, in the 1890s, exerting most of its efforts to control an influx of Orientals to the West Coast.

On the West Coast some people said: Let's keep out the "Yellow Peril," first the Chinese and then the Japanese. And many a Bostonian cursed the Irish when they came there.

As wave after wave of immigrants reached the United States those who were already here cried out in alarm. They feared the alien "hordes," the "torrential tides," the "silent invasions." And all the pejoratives flung in former years against the Russians, Czechs, Poles, Chinese, Irish, and Italians today are hurled against the Mexicans.

Immigration is not peculiar to this country. In Europe after the second World War, thousands of Yugoslavs, Greeks, Turks, Portuguese, and Spaniards emigrated to Germany, Switzerland, and France. Thousands of Africans came from Morocco and Libya to Spain and Italy.

Thousands of Indians and Pakistanis came to England. Like the Mexicans coming to the United States, these were laborers in search of better economic opportunities. They took any job at any pay. And even though they were contributing to the economic growth of Europe, they were forced to endure antagonism from those who did not like their drive and their spirit. Then, with the rise of unemployment in the 1970s, they were met with exclusion and deportation.

Beyond Europe there are similar examples. The Chinese have been emigrating to Indonesia and Malaysia for hundreds of years. Indians have been emigrating to Burma, Cambodia, and East Africa. And all have known what it is to be discriminated against in the lands where they have settled.

Nor is emigration entirely unknown to the United States. All of us who were born in this country know friends who have gone to live in other countries. I have a sister who lives in Greece. Another sister and her husband live half of each year in Mexico. A cousin lives in Afghanistan. Many of those with whom I grew up in the United States now have scattered throughout the world. Citizens of the United States can easily get visas to go almost anywhere. And we accept this freedom for ourselves as natural.

We also assume it is natural for Puerto Ricans to want to come and go from their island to the mainland. We were quick to welcome Cubans fleeing from Castro and Hungarians who fled Communism. More recently we've been giving residence visas to thousands of Vietnamese. We view political motivations very differently from economic, however. Somehow we feel different about the Mexicans.

Pressures for new restrictive measures against undocumented workers are based on three principal assumptions, according to Alberto Juárez of the Los Angeles

One-Stop Immigration Center, a legal-aid office for Mexicans. These are:

First, that the illegals displace large numbers of United States workers.

Second, that the low-cost labor of illegals is worth less than what they get in welfare and other social services.

Third, that the illegals all want to settle here permanently.

"No one has evidence to support any of these assumptions," Juárez said. "Studies show that Mexican workers take the jobs that whites and blacks in this country will not take. If the Mexican worker weren't there to do them, the chances are the jobs would go begging."

Studies have shown that Mexican illegals make amazingly little use of tax-supported social services while they are in the United States and that the cost of the services they do use is far outweighed by their contributions to Social Security and income tax revenues.

Robert A. Malson of the Domestic Policy Staff at the White House told me: "Data do not support the theory that illegal aliens are a burden to welfare."

A study sponsored by the County of San Diego, and written up by Vic Villalponde, concluded: "Undocumented workers are not flocking to this country to get on welfare. In San Diego, of 9,132 welfare recipients evaluated over a seven month period in 1975, only 10 undocumented immigrants were shown to be receiving welfare benefits.

"In a similar investigation of 14,000 cases, the County of Los Angeles found that 56 undocumented aliens were receiving welfare benefits, of which 54 were found to be officially eligible for assistance under present regulations."

Studies also do not bear out the third fear of many Americans: that the illegals come here to take up permanent residence and thus burden our society. This is true in the case of many white illegals who cut home ties and cross oceans to get here. It is not true, however, in the case of most Mexican workers. We ourselves set a migratory pattern for them when we instigated the bracero program recruiting workers, never settlers, who came for specified jobs and who returned to Mexico once the jobs were finished.

President Carter has proposed amnesty for those illegals who have resided in this country for seven consecutive years. This will not benefit many Mexicans—perhaps five percent of the illegals who are here. Relatively few have been here for seven years without returning to Mexico.

Too many Americans fall into two camps: those able to "prove" we are running out of jobs and oil and clean air, and those able to "prove" our population can grow many times over and still not affect our standard of living.

We are still a young, growing nation. Charles Abrams, who was New York's Housing Commissioner and wrote extensively on that subject, once made the point that everyone in the United States could live in California within sight of the ocean and they would not be as crowded as some people now are in New York City.

Thomas Jefferson wrote that the potential for population growth was one of the greatest assets our nation had for the future. He drew up a table projecting what the population growth could be and was very nearly right. Without that growth in population he knew America would be one of the lesser powers.

Besides being a young nation, we are a rich nation: We own some 48 percent of the world's wealth yet we have only 6 percent of the population. Our birthrate is now down to the point where we are not reproducing ourselves: the average woman does not have the 2.15 children necessary to simply maintain the population at a steady level. Some experts now remind us that with our declining birthrate, the end of unlimited legal immigration, and a labor force that is selective in its work, we need the Mexicans more than ever.

Meanwhile, however, we are deploying Vietnam veterans, tons of surplus material from the Vietnam War, and the same Vietnam "logic": Sophisticated weapons can defeat the desperation of poverty. In a real sense, then, we did not leave Vietnam; we brought it home with us.

Two thousand Border Patrolmen, more sensors, more night-seeing telescopes, and more helicopters all have been ordered in 1978 for our border with Mexico. But these will be no more of a solution to this war against the illegals than they were in Vietnam.

This is not a paramilitary problem. It is a human problem and a rural problem. The proposals by the Carter Administration calling for stricter security measures and fines for employers who knowingly hire undocumented workers are designed to treat symptoms and do nothing to cure the disease.

The solution lies south of the border, and the best people in the White House, Congress, and executive agencies will have to join with the best people in the Mexican government or we will be in a disaster together. It must be a labor-intensive solution, and it must be village-based.

The key long-range ingredient in any proposal to solve the Mexican illegal alien problem is to provide more work and better living conditions in the villages of Mexico.

"You had the Marshall Plan for Germany after the war, and you even helped Japan," Tijuana's mayor, Fernando Márquez-Arce, said, "The least you can do now is help your neighbor."

A Border Patrol agent echoed the same sentiment when he told me: "We give financial assistance to

Vietnam and other countries ... we can do the same for our neighbor."

New York's Senator Jacob Javits has called for a $250 billion, ten-year "world Marshall Plan"—in which Mexico would be included—to lift countries out of a world depression. He said unemployment and economic stagnation in other countries could create "grave danger" in our own country.

Before beginning any such program of foreign aid, however, we need to realize that what worked in the cities of Germany and Japan is *not* what is needed in Mexico. Our problem is illegal immigration and their problem is urbanization. These problems do *not* start in the cities, they arise in the countryside and the villages. The solution must start there.

There has been an enormous flow of United States investment dollars to Mexican manufacturing since the 1940s and it continues up to the present time. New industrialization in Mexico has been mostly for consumer goods and has been controlled by foreign-owned multinational corporations. This kind of economic development has not been able—nor will it ever be able—to solve the basic problems of poverty and backwardness in large parts in Mexico.

Industrialization has been what economists call an "import substituting industrialization," that is, a process by which firms in Mexico, many of them owned or controlled directly by U.S. companies, simply set up and produce consumer goods locally that were previously imported from the United States.

This means that rich people in Mexico and the United States join together to produce consumer goods that only the affluent can buy.

But most of the Mexicans are desperately poor. They are rural peasants. They barely eke out an existence on

the land. When radio and television tell them of a better
life to be had, they go in search of it. They swarm into
Mexico City and along our border. They are unskilled and
starving. Because they are starving, they are politically
and socially unstable. They beg for any job as domestic
servants and bootblacks, and everywhere they are street
vendors. It is not enough to talk glibly of giving economic
aid, without seeing where it will be directed. Industrialization of the cities and the exploitation of natural
resources by multinational corporations will only attract
more migrants. And the world is less in need of what
they can produce in the city than the agricultural
production of the villages where people now live.

Many so-called "technological advances" are the worst
possible innovations in a country such as Mexico. Mexico
needs oil production, steel, and computers. But it also
needs the philosophy "Small is Beautiful." It needs
factories for those now in the cities. But it also needs
village cooperatives, where a tractor and fertilizer and
seed shared by many can greatly enhance production and
cottage industries can improve the quality of life for all.
And it needs marketing, pricing mechanisms, credit
policies, and political systems to support that effort.

Mexico must create jobs in city and village for a
multitude. But rather than our sophisticated technology,
the country needs large-scale planning to keep villagers
on the land. It needs carefully designed programs of rural
development and job creation.

Mexico's President López Portillo frankly acknowl-
edges the problem of the illegals is due "to the lack of
work in Mexico. We know it is the obligation of Mexico to
find enough work for our citizens. We are doing what we
can."

However, the Mexican president adds, there are things
the United States can do to help stimulate the Mexican

economy. "We are a nation that produces many things we could sell to the United States. But as of now our level of trade with you is very poor. We want to bring it up to a higher level."

Police are not the answer to the alien problem, López Portillo says. "We see it as a problem of commerce, a problem of finance, a problem of demography ... we cannot resolve it as a police problem."

The writer-historian Carey McWilliams points out there is little prospect that the Mexican immigrant, legal or illegal, ever will achieve anything approximating economic and social equality in this country until conditions in his homeland change for the better.

McWilliams, who wrote *North from Mexico*, one of the most comprehensive academic reviews of this problem, says the solution must lie in mutual efforts by both countries. "Labor intensive agriculture developments in Mexico would be a good thing and would help a lot," he says. "But it will require a great deal of cooperation between Mexico and the United States. They can't export their problems to the United States and on the other hand we can't close the border. So the only answer is intensive, continuous good faith and cooperation, not only on one level but on many levels."

McWilliams emphasizes that all other measures being proposed—identity cards, fines for employers who knowingly hire undocumented workers—all of these "will not do the trick," because they deal with peripheral aspects and in many cases may actually exacerbate the problem. "This other approach, working with Mexico, has to happen," he stresses.

"The flow is still great, the Mexican nationals are still coming and the United States still has a very confused policy," Immigration Commissioner Castillo says. "That's because nobody will agree on it.

"We deport some people 20 times. We have a revolving door and we're the person who spins it. The United States has to have a policy."

Our choices are really quite simple if you look at them in human terms, Castillo continues. "Aside from the legalities and the national and international policy questions, in *human* terms we now have several million people in the United States who are subject to exploitation, abuse, misuse, harassment, and who live in constant fear. This can't continue."

Castillo favors working out a plan whereby those who are working illegally can work legally.

This would not necessarily mean granting citizenship. Mexico itself does not want to lose its citizens. But it wants them to have the right to come here to work—on a temporary basis, as millions have traditionally done.

It seems to me that the bracero-type approach we had in the past—that allows workers to come here legally—is better than what we now have: workers who come here illegally.

Meanwhile, we continue to spend at least $250 million on our no-win war against the undocumented workers. There is the cost of parole and probation, and of incarceration in city and county jails, in four detention camps, and in our federal prisons. Two of the latter, La Tuna near El Paso and one in Stafford, Arizona, are almost entirely for illegals. Then there are the huge costs of all the deportation hearings. In addition are the costs of transporting thousands of men from one jail to another.

An average Mexican illegal could feed his family for a month for what it costs us to keep him in detention for one day. Tens of thousands of landless Mexican farmers earn less than $75 a year. Yet, when we lock one up, it costs us an average of $22 a day or about $8,000 per year in prison costs alone.

The millions we spend on protecting our border, sending work-hungry Mexicans to prison or deporting them, could more profitably be spent in creating jobs to keep them in Mexico.

In the nineteenth century, we took land—from Texas to California—as part of our Manifest Destiny. We also got the Spanish-speaking people who were living on that vast Mexican territory. And others who would come later. The people, as well as the land, we now must realize, are part of our destiny.

Walt Whitman foresaw a long time ago the influence the Spanish-speaking people would bring to our lives. In 1883 he wrote: "To that composite American identity of the future, Spanish character will supply some of the most needed parts. No stock shows a grander historic retrospect—grander in religiousness and loyalty, or for patriotism, courage, decorum, gravity and honor."

To the roster of qualities Whitman attributes to Spanish-speaking people—and I think now of the Mexicans—I would add a sense of joy and happiness. I think of the six-year-old Jesús who shined my shoes in a Reynosa park: "Me *happy*," he said, flashing a radiant smile, "You happy, too?" And I think of a 17-year-old illegal in tattered clothes and floppy shoes in one of our jails. "We Mexicans," he told me, his one good eye bright with his zest for life, "work harder than the Anglos." And I recall Lola, a farm worker: "I want to live life intensely, passionately." And she does. Against all odds.

Most of the Mexican illegals we arrest are what we would call simple people. This has certain advantages. They have not as yet been moulded by modern industrialism. They are a people, as the Spanish poet Federico García Lorca put it, "with their hearts in their heads."

The Mexicans in this country generally have known every difficulty, every hardship, every suffering. Yet they bravely see joy as an object of life. They speak up for joy in their music, in their dance, in their literature, their poetry—and in their ability to see any work, well done, as honorable work.

If we as a nation are to be invaded by the Mexicans, let us hope they bequeath the rest of us this sense of joy.

Many years ago Senator William Borah said all that ever need be said about relations between the United States and Mexico and our respective peoples:

"God has made us neighbors; let justice make us friends."